W9-AEI-916

Newton Center

100/164

Pierre Teilhard de Chardin
HIS THOUGHT

CARMELITE MONASTERY
1381 UNIVERSITY AVE.
NEW YORK 10452 N. Y.

Pierre Teilhard de Chardin
HIS THOUGHT

by Claude Tresmontant

with a Preface by Gustave Weigel, S.J.

1959 · HELICON PRESS · BALTIMORE

DC
215.07
T

Introduction à la pensée de Pierre Teilhard de Chardin was published in Paris by Éditions du Seuil. This translation was made by Salvator Attanasio.

Nihil obstat: EDWARD A. CERNY, S.S., D.D.
      Censor librorum

Imprimatur: † FRANCIS P. KEOUGH, D.D.
      Archbishop of Baltimore
      October 8, 1959

© 1959 by Helicon Press, Inc., Baltimore 27

LIBRARY OF CONGRESS CATALOG CARD NUMBER: 59-14334

PRINTED IN THE UNITED STATES OF AMERICA BY NORTH CENTRAL PUBLISHING COMPANY, ST. PAUL, MINNESOTA

Preface

BY GUSTÄVE WEIGEL, S.J.

This book deals with the thought of Père Pierre Teilhard de Chardin, S.J. Since he was not too well known in America where he died, it may not be an impudence first of all to advise the English-speaking reader that "Teilhard" is pronounced "Tay—áhr."

Obviously more must be said. In saying it I do not hope to rival Claude Cuénot's biography of Teilhard de Chardin, *Pierre Teilhard de Chardin. Les grandes étapes de son évolution* (Paris: Plon, 1958), nor imitate the highly enthusiastic foreword of Sir Julian Huxley to Teilhard de Chardin's *The Phenomenon of Man* (tr. by Bernard Wall; New York: Harper, 1959). I shall say only a few words to give the reader some basic facts concerning Père Teilhard's life and work.

Marie-Joseph-Pierre Teilhard de Chardin was born on May 1, 1881, at Sarcenat, D'Orcines, near Clermont-Ferrand, France. The family belonged to the *petite noblesse* and were well-to-do. In 1892 he was admitted to the Jesuit college of Notre Dame de Mongré at Villefranche-sur-Saône. Here he was an outstanding pupil and became prefect of the sodality of our Lady, for as a classmate later stated, he was a model student and of great piety. At the age of seventeen he had already decided to become a Jesuit and he entered the order on March 20, 1899, in the novitiate and juniorate at Aix-en-Provence.

He made the usual studies required by the Jesuit Order. His philosophical and scientific training was at the Jesuit house on the English Isle of Jersey, beyond France but near it. Even during high school Teilhard had been interested in geology and this interest deepened on the Isle of Jersey. At the end of philosophy (1905) he was sent to the Jesuit college in Cairo, where he taught chemistry and physics. Here he became passionately devoted to the study of paleontology. In 1908 he began his theology at the French Jesuit house, Ore Place, Hastings (Sussex), in England. After his third of four years of divinity he was ordained to the priesthood on August 24, 1911. During this time Teilhard's interest in geology and paleontology not only survived but became sound and scholarly.

Finishing theology in 1912, Teilhard went to Paris for formal training in paleontology. 1914 brought the First World War and the paleontologist joined the French Army as a stretcher-bearer. His bravery was recognized and he won the *croix de guerre* and the *médaille militaire*. While still in military service, and with no Tertianship made, Teilhard was allowed to make his solemn profession in the Society of Jesus at Lyons, May 26, 1918.

After the war he continued his studies in paleontology and prehistory. He received his doctorate triumphantly at the University of Paris in 1922. He was not only studying at this time but also teaching geology at the Institut Catholique of Paris. In 1923 he went to China where he stayed until 1927 with a two-year interlude in Paris. In 1927 he went to French Somaliland and Ethiopia. In 1929 he went back to China where he took part in various paleontological expeditions in Manchuria and the Gobi desert. From 1932 to 1938 he worked in and around Peking. After a stay in the United States and France during 1938–39, he returned to Peking in 1939 to stay in China until 1946. In that year he returned to Paris where he stayed until 1951. He then visited South Africa and passed over to South America on his way to New York in 1951 where he was to spend his last years with the Wenner-Gren Foundation for Anthropological Research.

On Easter Day, April 10, 1955, he died suddenly. After a simple funeral his remains were buried at the Jesuit Novitiate, St. Andrew-on-Hudson, Poughkeepsie, N. Y.

This rapid list of times and places says very little about the man. It does show that he lived all over the world. Of course in all his journeys outside of France he worked in paleontology and anthropology. He was recognized as one of the leading men in these fields. His written works are many. He knew all the savants who were interested in the story and meaning of man, and he was admired and loved by them: Abbé Henri Breuil, Lucien Cuénot, Sir Charles Dawson, E. A. Hooten, Sir Julian Huxley, Édouard Le Roy, Henry Fairchild Osborn, Sven Hedin, Arnold Toynbee, and many others.

But the significance of Teilhard de Chardin does not consist primarily in his great merits as an anthropologist or paleontologist. Though probably he did more to confirm the theory of evolution by his paleontological findings than any other man in our time, his interests were larger than paleontology. Teilhard was a deep thinker and a man of profound Catholic piety. The vision that he had achieved was one of the synthesis of all reality: material, biological, psychological, sociological and religious. The dynamic idea to organize this ambitious synthesis was the notion of evolution as a transcendental force operating as an instrument of God. He worked with the theologians and he himself was deeply interested in theology. He did not meet with much enthusiasm from the theological brotherhood which felt that his synthesis was too revolutionary; neither did it feel that the evolutionary concept was a secure basis from which to work. Père Teilhard could not get his work published in his lifetime because of this theological opposition. It was only after his death that his friends gathered his writings and published them on their own responsibility.

Whether or not Teilhard's massive, complex and original vision will remake the philosophy and theology of our schools

vii

is a question which cannot be answered at this moment.

He may sink into momentary oblivion to be discovered at a more propitious date; or his work, genial as it is, may only remain an isolated effort in the history of human thought. Whatever be the ultimate fate of Père Teilhard's vision of the cosmos, it certainly has a grandeur which will impress the reader and give him furiously to think.

Contents

Preface   v

Introduction   3

PART ONE: The Vision of the World   11

    I. Point of View and Method   13
    II. The Direction of Evolution   18
    III. The Yardstick of Growing Complexity   23
    IV. The Yardstick of Cephalization   32
    V. Evolution Continues   36
    VI. The Step Toward Reflection   40
    VII. The Convergence of Evolution   50
    VIII. The Omega Point   58

PART TWO: Teilhard, Christian Thinker   65

    IX. Christology   67
    X. Spirituality   78
    XI. *Quaestiones Disputatae*   89
    XII. Conclusions and Reflections   99

Glossary   107

Bibliography   112

Indices   127

Introduction

It is useful to distinguish in the work of Teilhard de Chardin various planes or levels which are distinct, but not separate, from one another.

There is, first of all, the technical work of Teilhard the paleontologist.[1] Then again there is what can be called Teilhard de Chardin's "phenomenology." This is a scientific synthesis, a vision of the world which came to the eminent scientist in the course of the forty years of research and reflection which he devoted to an attempt to decipher the totality of spatio-temporal phenomena at a scientific level.

Finally there is Teilhard de Chardin's theology, Christology, spirituality and mysticism.

As we have said, these planes and levels are distinct from one another; but it should be clearly understood that Teilhard's paleontological research served as a basis for his vision of the world, his *Weltanshauung*. This scientific discovery of the universe forced Teilhard to rethink his Christianity. As a result he was able to develop, at the same time, a positive scientific knowledge of the world and an understanding of the mystery of Christ. This very attempt to achieve a total synthesis characterizes Teilhard's work at its best.

In the process, however, Teilhard rigorously satisfied epistemological requirements on each plane of discourse and in each order of research. His was not an attempt to effect a contrived

---

[1] Cf. "Titres et travaux de Pierre Teilhard de Chardin," a mimeographed bibliography published on the occasion of his election to the Collège de France. See also Jean Piveteau, "L'œuvre paléontologique du P. Teilhard de Chardin," *Quaternaria*, Rome, 1955.

harmony, but a quest for coherence and a unity that was at the same time cognizant of the diversity which was attendant upon the advance of knowledge.

This study will not be concerned with Teilhard's strictly technical and paleontological writings. A study of this fundamental part of his work can be made only by a specialist in the field. Our aim is to draw up a balance sheet of Teilhard's "philosophical" and "spiritual" work, and of his contribution as a Christian thinker. Let us agree that the term "philosophical" shall here be accorded the broad meaning of "philosophy of nature," i.e., scientific phenomenology.

We shall not attempt to retrace the "evolution" of Teilhard's thought, nor the development of his insights and major theses as these came into being in the course of research. Nor shall we chronologically follow the progress of his synthesis and its clarification. Naturally such an undertaking would be of great interest, and someday it will certainly have to be made. It would require, however, a descriptive presentation of Teilhard's thought as it appeared in his very first essay: at a time, that is, when it was least clear in formulation, least scientific in approach, and, in general, most debatable. This is a task for a historian whose efforts will be properly rewarded if he focuses attention on the very development of Teilhard's doctrine. Such a study, it really need not be said, would be of great psychological interest.

But this method, which would require a retracing of the long path followed by Teilhard before he arrived at a definitive expression of his thought, has its disadvantages at the moment. Teilhard's thought is not sufficiently well known (and this is, of course, the chief disadvantage) to justify a historical investigation of this kind.

Thus it appears more appropriate to present Teilhard's thought in its final form, in its fullness of expression, and in its scientific maturity. Naturally, we also shall have to mention the history or genesis of this or that Teilhardian idea or insight, recalling its earliest formulation and following it through its growth and development.

We shall give preference, as we have explained, to Teilhard's mature writings in which he reached the acme of his development.

This method is the more justifiable in the case of Teilhard because, on the whole, he remained remarkably faithful to his first vision of things. This vision of the world was enriched and nourished by the scientific and technical argumentation Teilhard brought to it. In the course of time it became more precise, but it never underwent a fundamental change. There are not several "epochs," several "philosophies" in his thought, as in Schelling's for example.

On the other hand, over a period of forty years during which he wrote some two hundred essays, Teilhard, like Leibniz, did repeat himself. But he did not remain static; every repetition was a step forward. In this way he further developed his initial intuition, digging ever deeper and becoming ever more precise in the elaboration of his rigorously scientific vision. One might say that Teilhard did not so much write two hundred essays as begin the same essay over and over again, two hundred times, until his dying day.

Therefore our greatest interest lies in the consideration of Father Teilhard's thought in its final form, but at the same time we shall make use of his earlier essays in order to clarify the genesis of the ideas discussed.

Our harvest is gathered mainly from the works of Teilhard's last fifteen years. Only after the completion of *Le phénomène humain* (1940) did Teilhard come into full possession of his vision of the world. It was only after this time that he wrote his principal texts and masterpieces.

The development is less clear in his writings that can be termed "spiritual." *Le milieu divin* (1927) is indubitably one of his masterpieces. But it was to his scientific synthesis especially, as is natural, that Teilhard was constantly adding im-

provements. This does not mean that there was no steady
progression in his spiritual, his mystical, life to the very end.
Indeed, his love for Christ was ever on the increase. But his
mystical vision of the world was less subject to change than his
scientific explorations; and this is what we might have expected.

If we except his purely technical studies, Teilhard's work is
one long series of essays stretching from 1916 to 1955, the year
of his death.

On the whole these essays are short; some consist of only a
few pages. The longest essay is *Le phénomène humain*. Teilhard
preferred to express himself in brief essays; from year to year he
would return to them and revise. For the most part his essays
are still unpublished, though some have appeared in *Études* or
in *Revue des questions scientifiques*, in *Annales de paléontologie* and elsewhere.

Their nonpublication, perhaps, explains why they were constantly revised, according to circumstances, and why the same
ideas were often repeated in his published essays, lectures and
even in his correspondence. Again Leibniz comes to mind.

Friends very early mimeographed Father Teilhard's writings.

In line with Bergson's advice in such matters, we should ask
the following questions: What was the original intuition which
sparked Teilhard's total vision of the world? What was the
initial "contact" from which all his thought received its *élan* and
inspiration? And, finally, what was the first "negation" which
determined the main affirmations of his work?

Nothing less than a study of all his works in their complete
development would be required in order to get at the germ, the
spiritual contact, in the very heart of Teilhard's thought. But
what is important for us to know are those ideas which Teilhard
developed and clarified up to the end of his life. Only at the
very end of this presentation will it be possible to ask the further
questions: What is the center from which his total vision radi-
ates? What is the unique thing which this "philosopher" strove
to express in the multiplicity of his writings?

Fortunately, in Teilhard's case, we possess an "inner" history, a spiritual autobiography which helps to shed some light on the psychological origin of his work. It retraces the genesis of his vision of the world. This text, "Le cœur de la matière," is dated 1950: appropriate as it may be to refer to it, we must bear in mind that the inner happenings described actually took place long before the publication date. In this text it is an old man who is describing the evolution of his vision from his childhood days onward. But the remembrances are so clear, so compellingly vivid that their fidelity to truth is beyond question.

In a text dated 1917, Teilhard already revealed a characteristic peculiar to the inner life of his childhood:

From my earliest childhood the need to possess some "absolute" was the pivot of all my inner life. Amid the pleasures which surrounded me at this age, I was happy only (I remember it vividly) when I felt fundamental joy which, in general, consisted in the possession (or the thought) of some object sensed to be more precious, more consistent, and more unalterable than any other. Sometimes it was just a piece of metal; or again, leaping to the other extreme, I would take delight in the thought of God/Spirit (at that time, the Flesh of Christ seemed to me too fragile, too corruptible).

This preoccupation may seem singular. But I repeat that it was ever the case with me. I had at that time an irresistible need (both life-giving and consoling) to come to rest forever in something tangible and definite. And I searched everywhere for this beatifying Object. The story of my inner life is summed up in this search, ever dwelling on realities more and more universal and perfect. Fundamentally this deep natural tendency has remained absolutely unchanged ever since I began to know myself.[2]

The same recollections were more clearly expressed in "Le cœur de la matière" in 1950:

As a point of departure, a guiding thread, and as an axis of continuity to everything which is to follow, I feel I must first of all describe a particular psychological tendency or "polarization," common indeed to all persons (although it is not always clearly recognized by them) which, for lack of a better term, I shall call the "sense of plenitude." As far back as I can go in remembrance of my child-

[2] "Mon univers," 1917.

hood, nothing has seemed to me more familiarly characteristic of my inner life than my taste or irresistible need for some all-encompassing, unique entity, sufficient and necessary in and to itself. A need to be fully at ease, to be completely happy, to know that "something essential" exists, something of which all else is but an adjunct or an ornament. To know "something" of this existent and to enjoy the knowledge thereof endlessly! In fact if, upon reviewing my past life, I manage somehow to recognize myself and retrace my path, I can do so only by following the trail of this particular note, nuance, or taste which, once it has been felt, can never be confused with any other emotion, whether it be the joy of knowledge, or discovery, of creation, or of love. And this, not so much because it is different from them as for the reason that it is an order higher than all these emotions, but in which, nonetheless, they are all contained.

Teilhard's early works are metaphysical, mystical and sometimes even *too* poetical in character. Written during the First World War, they appear old-fashioned to minds steeped in critical analysis. They are, indeed, reminiscent of the metaphysical speculations of the seventeenth century. One can easily imagine a correspondence between Leibniz and the Teilhard of this period, like the correspondence between Leibniz and Father des Bosses on the subject of the *"Vinculum substantiale."*

These early essays are of interest primarily because they reveal Teilhard's first beliefs in their pure, simple form; they project his first vision of the world, not yet condensed and distilled. Teilhard's extensive scientific training, of course, played a part in the development of these speculations on creation, evil, the plurality of inhabited worlds, original sin, the One and the Many, in their proper places. Gradually, however, Teilhard came into possession of his own method, his "order" of scientific research.

Thereafter he departed but rarely from this method, strictly scientific and phenomenological. Metaphysical "speculations" were to occupy only a very slight place in his work. Teilhard expressed his metaphysical ideas only very rarely and then only in an appendix, in his correspondence or in conversation. He was to make the "physical (in the broadest sense of the term) order" of investigation uniquely his.

Teilhard's first scientific essays were written in 1923: "L'hominisation" (used by É. Le Roy in *Les Origines humaines et l'Évolution de l'intelligence*), and the article "La paléontologie et l'apparition de l'homme," which appeared in *La revue de philosophie*.

PART I

THE VISION OF THE WORLD

CHAPTER I

Point of View and Method

Teilhard de Chardin's point of view is scientific and phenomenological. It was formulated as early as 1916 in an essay, which in other respects can be termed metaphysical and mystical, and which announced a theme his later work was to make somewhat more specific. Teilhard evoked "the law of recurrence in accordance with which the cosmos is structured. The analysis of matter leads the investigator to view it as an innumerable aggregate of centers which capture and dominate one another in such a way that, by their combinations, they build centers of a higher order and increasing complexity" ("La vie cosmique," 1916).

However, the first of his essays which was strictly scientific in its method appeared in 1923: "The following pages do not seek to present any philosophy directly; on the contrary, they claim to derive their authority from the care that has been taken to avoid any recourse to metaphysics. What they propose to do is to express a vision, as objective and simple as possible, of humanity considered as a *phenomenon* in its totality and its connections with the universe" ("L'hominisation," 1923).

Long extracts from this unpublished essay can be found in the book by Édouard Le Roy mentioned in the Introduction.

Teilhard formulated the same methodological principles in many of his later writings. In 1937, in his "Esquisse d'un univers personnel," he stated: "Never has the notion of an Absolute Good, of causality, or finality been introduced in the development of our thesis either explicitly or implicitly. What we present to the positivist philosophy of our century is an experimental law, a rule of succession within duration."

13

In 1942, in the Preface to his important essay entitled, "La place de l'homme dans l'univers, réflexions sur la complexité," Teilhard wrote:

First, it should be well understood that in the following pages I shall, as is proper, stick to the terrain of facts, i.e., to the realm of the tangible and to that which can be photographed. Discussing scientific perspectives as a scientist I must and shall restrict myself to the investigation of the arrangement of appearances, that is, of "phenomena." Since my concern is with their connections and with the succession manifested by these phenomena, I shall not deal with their underlying causalities. Perhaps I may go so far as to hazard an "ultraphysics." But no one should look for metaphysics here.

In 1944, in his "Centrologie," he declared: "Here is no a priori geometric synthesis proceeding from a definition of being, but an experimental *law of recurrence*, verifiable in the phenomenal sphere and which can be properly extrapolated to the totality of space and time. Thus here is no abstract metaphysics, but a realistic ultraphysics of union."

The same definition of his point of view and method was repeated during an important lecture Teilhard delivered in 1945 (published as "Vie et planètes," *Études* [May, 1946]): "It must be stated beforehand that in this lecture — during which there will be no straying from the scientific terrain of observation — only the succession and the interdependence of phenomena are to be considered, i.e., only the *experimental law of recurrence*. Thus there will be no ontological analysis of causes."

In this connection the Preface to *Le phénomène humain*, which appeared in 1947, is of capital importance:

In order to be properly understood this book must be read, not as a metaphysical work, and still less as a sort of theological essay, but simply and solely as a scientific dissertation. This is indicated by the very title. The book treats man *solely* as a phenomenon, but it also treats of the *whole* phenomenon of man.

First and foremost it treats of man solely as a phenomenon. No one should look here for an explanation, but only for an introduction to an explanation, of the world. I have merely tried to establish around man, chosen as a center, a coherent order between consequences and antecedents. I have not tried to discover a system of ontological relations between the elements of the universe, but instead an experimental law of recurrence expressing their successive appearance in the course of time. Beyond this first scientific reflection there is, of course, plenty of room for the most far-ranging reflections of the philosopher and the theologian. I have at all times carefully avoided venturing forth into the realm of being in its deepest sense. At the most, I trust, that on the plane of experience I have perceived with some accuracy the combined movement toward unity, and that I have also properly marked off those places where philosophical and religious thinkers, in their further investigations, and for reasons of a higher order, would be justified to look for gaps in the continuity.

But this book also treats of the *whole* phenomenon of man. It is just this, however, which, without contradicting what I have just said (though it may appear to do so), risks giving to the views suggested here the *appearance* of philosophy. . . .

Further on, Teilhard returns to the delimitation of his viewpoint, described as

an effort to see and to show what man becomes and requires when he is placed entirely within the framework of appearances. I repeat that in these pages my only aim — on which I have exerted my full energies — is simply *to see* or in other words, to develop a *homogeneous* and *coherent* perspective of our general extended experience of man. A *whole* which enfolds. Thus no one should look here for a final explanation of things — a metaphysics.

In 1948, in a text entitled "Résumé de la pensée du Père," Teilhard defined his work as a "phenomenology": "Essentially P. Teilhard de Chardin's thought is not expressed in a metaphysics, but in a sort of phenomenology. He thinks that a certain law of recurrence, the law of complexity/consciousness, which fuses and dominates all experience, compels our observation."

Finally, in the series of lectures given at the Sorbonne on the human zoological group: its structure and evolutive directions, Teilhard reaffirmed the purely scientific character of his efforts.

As indicated by the title, the following pages do not claim to give an exhaustive definition of man. Their aim is merely to fix man's "phenomenal" appearances to the extent (as regards our terrestrial observation) that the human element can legitimately be viewed by science as a prolongation and the crown, at least provisionally, of the living element. Thus the well-circumscribed aim of this work is an attempt to define this mysterious human phenomenon experimentally by fixing its present position, structurally and historically, in relation to the other forms around us which the cosmic stuff has assumed in the course of time.

We have felt obliged to cite these texts, spread out over different periods of Teilhard's activity, as proof of Teilhard's awareness of being engaged in a strictly scientific enterprise. To be sure, the vision of the world thus disclosed is of philosophical import and value, but it commits the philosopher only to the extent that it has been formulated by means, and according to methods, rigorously free from any extrascientific presuppositions.

This order of scientific and phenomenological investigation was Teilhard's proper sphere, and in this he excelled. Teilhard was very much aware of the fact that he was, above all, a "physician" or natural philosopher in the broad sense of the term: "I am neither a philosopher nor a theologian, but a student of the 'phenomenon,' a physicist in the old Greek sense."[1]

In a remarkable essay, Msgr. Bruno de Solages has rightly emphasized Teilhard's specific point of view, and criticized the misinterpretations that frequently arise in this connection:

At a first reading a person, whose mind has been formed primarily by the scholastic disciplines customary in the seminaries, is easily disconcerted. Such a person wonders what it is that he is dealing with: Is it science? Is it philosophy? Is it theology? According to the question he poses, the reader is tempted to reproach the author for not explaining himself on this or that theological question or, on

---

[1] *Nouvelles lettres de voyage*, Jan. 11, 1951. See also "La réflexion de l'énergie," *Revue des questions scientifiques* (Oct., 1952), p. 482: "Our investigation which is situated on the plane of 'appearances' does not deal with the transcendental problem of causality."

the contrary, to reproach him for mixing all perspectives — unless he is hypnotized by the magnificent drapery in which this thought is enveloped, and views it only as a kind of poetry. All these errors of interpretation have a common source: The reader of Teilhard's texts does not place himself on the same plane of observation with them. For no matter how it might appear to certain people, Teilhard is perfectly aware of his aim and method, of the plane on which he moves, and of the angle from which he tackles the real. The splendor of the form must not throw us off the track: we are in the presence of an extremely rigorous dialectic.

What, then, is the point of view? . . . To the extent that so modern a thought can be enclosed in ancient frames, it must be said that his fundamental point of view is what Aristotle called physics and the scholastics call cosmology. In its consideration of the totality of reality, the point of view is the objective view of science. It aims to present a systematic exposition of this total reality and to sort out its essential laws and those pertaining to the existence of God. Did not Aristotle himself, beginning with the Eighth Book of his *Physics,* introduce proof for the existence of the first unmoved Mover? [2]

In a recent book, François Meyer has analyzed the epistemological problems posed by a "phenomenology of evolution" at the microscopic level. He points out the inevitable resistance such a phenomenology is bound to encounter from specialists who work at the level of the microphenomenal. Meyer concludes, however, by asserting the legitimacy of a phenomenological reading at the level of the macrophenomenal, a reading which permits the sorting out of evolutive laws indiscernible at the microscopic level. This is the phenomenology which is the proper object of Teilhard's research. Meyer does not cite Teilhard, but from the methodological and epistemological point of view, Teilhard's work, it seems to us, appears to be confirmed by Meyer's. [3]

[2] Bruno de Solages, "La pensée chrétienne face à l'évolution," *Bulletin de littérature ecclésiastique* (Toulouse), 1947; the translation is based on that of Harry Blair in *Cross Currents,* Summer, 1951, pp. 27–28.

[3] *Problématique de l'évolution,* 1954. Reviewed by Teilhard in *Études* (May, 1955).

CHAPTER 2

The Direction of Evolution

Biological evolution, discovered in the last century, has taught philosophy the direction of time. Evolution in its full sense — i.e., extended to the whole of reality — means that reality did not appear at one stroke, instantly, as it were. On the contrary, reality is engaged in progressively inventing itself, a process which has been going on for several billion years. The concept of evolution means that we are not situated in a completed cosmos, but are caught up, instead, in a process of cosmogenesis.

Teilhard very early understood this cosmic significance of the concept of evolution, legitimately extended to the totality of the spatio-temporal phenomena. "It was during the years I was studying theology at Hastings," he writes, "that little by little the consciousness of a deep, ontological and total drift of the environing universe developed within me — much less as an abstract notion than as a *presence* — until it invaded my whole inner atmosphere." [1]

Throughout his entire work Teilhard never tires of repeating that this consciousness of time, i.e., of the evolutive nature of reality, is truly a fundamental revolution which has affected our view of the world for a century. This capital transformation in our representation of the world will have enormous consequences in physics, metaphysics and mysticism. After recognizing that the earth does not occupy the spatial center of the world, modern man — since the time of Galileo — has discovered that the universe is not simply a mass of completed things, fixed

[1] "Le cœur de la matière," 1950.

18

and immobile in an assigned place, or having only a cyclic motion. The universe, rather, is in the process of being brought into being.

One of the most curious among the intellectual phenomena produced during the last fifty years in the realm of scientific thought is certainly that of the gradual, irresistible invasion of the physical-chemical by history. The first elements of matter are exchanging their quasi-absolute mathematical condition for that of contingent and concrete reality; physics and chemistry, those branches of arithmetic, are gradually beginning to appear as the preliminary chapters of a "Natural History of the World." . . . What a reversal in our representation of the universe! [2]

Thus evolution is not simply identifiable with "transformism." It is not a scientific "theory." Evolution simply signifies that the universe is a temporal phenomenon: This is tantamount to saying that the universe is in the process of being born, of being created all around us. The scientific concept of evolution is the experimental reverse of the metaphysical concept of creation. Starting from the real, at a scientific level, we note that the universe is not "something placed there" once and for all, but a series of things which are in the process of being created, and which are derived from one another. How could the metaphysical conception of creation ever have been opposed to the scientific idea of evolution? Only through a double confusion! It may be gratuitously supposed that creation must have been an instantaneous operation; or else a metaphysical thesis, which ordinarily would not enter into the question, is surreptitiously introduced into the scientific concept of evolution: we think here of the ontological autonomy of this genesis. At the level of phenomena, where we find ourselves in science, all that the concept of evolution indicates is the temporality of the creation which is in the process of realizing itself under our very eyes. This is exactly Teilhard's view: "Evolution," he wrote, "is never 'creative' as science was once able to believe. As regards

[2] "Le groupe zoologique humain," a course given at the Sorbonne in 1949.

our experience, it is, rather, creation expressed in time and space." [3]

Evolution is "the expression of the structural law (at one and the same time the law of both 'being' and knowledge) by virtue of which *nothing, absolutely nothing* . . . would be able to enter our life and field of vision save *by way of birth*, which, in other words, is a synonym for the 'universal temporal-spatial interconnection' of phenomena." [4]

It was only in the nineteenth century, under the influence of biology, that the "irreversible coherence" of all that exists was discovered:

The least (whether in nature or position) molecule of carbon has a function in the whole sidereal process; as does also the least protozoa, structurally so knit in the web of life that, hypothetically, its existence could not be destroyed without *ipso facto* bringing about the destruction of the biosphere. *The distribution, succession and solidarity of objects are born of their concrescence in a common genesis.* Time and space are organically joined again in order, together, to weave the stuff of the universe.[5]

Thus in its full and complete sense evolution is not a "hypothesis." Undoubtedly, scientists will continue to discuss the *modalities* of biological evolution. But here and now the notion of evolution is beyond discussion because it represents a *dimension* — the temporal dimension — of reality. It is not a "system," but a general condition to which, henceforth, all theories, hypotheses and systems must submit and which they must satisfy if they are to be thinkable and true.[6]

All scientists are now in agreement upon the general fact that we are situated in an unfinished universe, one that is in the throes of birth. In short they are agreed upon the fact that there is *an* evolution. But there is no particular agreement on the question

[3] "La place de l'homme dans l'univers," 1942. For the relation between "evolution" and "creation," see C. Tresmontant, *Études de métaphysique biblique,* Paris, 1955.
[4] "Réflexions sur l'ultra-humain," 1950.
[5] *Le phénomène humain* (1955), p. 241.
[6] *Ibid.*

whether the evolution of this universe is oriented or directed toward something, whether, in other words, evolution has a direction.[7]

For many scientists, moreover, the question of direction seems to smack of metaphysics; it is one which, therefore, no longer belongs to the sphere of science. In his book, already cited here, François Meyer has analyzed the presuppositions underlying this notion. The fact is that integral scientific phenomenology, as modern psychology has already shown, implies this search for a direction. The scientific reading of the phenomena *is*, in itself, a search for direction. Teilhard's originality probably lies in the fact that he introduced this legitimate demand for an elucidation of direction into the realm of cosmogenesis, biogenesis and anthropogenesis.

"Of itself and in itself," writes Teilhard,

a cosmogenesis can assume all sorts of shapes. For example, it can be imagined, a priori, either as a disordered state of agitated elements in process of dissolution (pseudo-cosmogenesis), or, on the contrary, as a directed process (eu-cosmogenesis). A cosmogenesis of the latter sort, in turn, may be imagined as capable of propagating itself in all directions like a ray in an amorphous environment, or else like light in an anisotropic environment, finding itself polarized along certain leading axes.

In the experiential reality of things, with which of these types of evolution are we dealing?

It does not seem as though science has yet taken an explicitly definite position on this important question, which inevitably will not be able to wait too long for an answer. Implicitly, however, it seems to me that, without doubt, science, with all its weight, is already orienting itself toward the recognition and admission of a *directed* cosmogenesis: this latter being ultimately defined by a principal axis of complexity/consciousness (or of "corpusculization") which traverses it.[8]

Teilhard's entire scientific work can be characterized as an effort to read the direction of evolution in reality itself, without

[7] "Esquisse d'un univers personnel," 1936; *Le phénomène humain*, p. 153.
[8] "Réflexions sur l'ultra humain," 1950.

recourse to any metaphysical presupposition, in order to elucidate its immanent intentionality in the very order of phenomena, and using the scientific method alone. Thus, in the realm of the total spatial-temporal phenomenon, Teilhard generalizes an advance, considered legitimate in other areas of knowledge, as in psychology, for example, as has been said.

"We find ourselves face to face with a problem of nature: to discover, *if such exists*, the direction of evolution. The question is to resolve this problem without straying from the realm of scientific facts. This is what I shall attempt to do here." [9]

This bold extension of the search for direction to the whole of the phenomenal world is necessary so that science may arrive at its normal terminus. It is, moreover, required so that human activity may find its full and complete justification, as we shall see later. "Science in its development and even mankind in its march, as I shall show later, are marking time at this moment because men's minds are disinclined to recognize that evolution has a precise *orientation* and a leading axis." [10]

[9] "Esquisse d'un univers personnel," 1936.
[10] *Le phénomène humain*, p. 154.

CHAPTER 3

The Yardstick of Growing Complexity

In order to discern the direction of evolution in the very order
of the phenomena, without straying from the scientific plane,
Teilhard applied himself to the task of sorting out a law of recurrence which would serve to define and measure the development
of the "cosmic stuff" in the course of time. Teilhard calls this
law of recurrence the law of complexity/consciousness. In the
course of time, matter has oriented itself toward more and more
complex and more and more improbable states. The emergence
of consciousness is found to be experimentally linked to the
increase in the complexity of the cosmic stuff.[1]

There is a cosmic drift of matter, which through entropy impels
itself forward, against the stream, toward combinations which are
more and more centro-complicated, combinations in the direction of
the "third infinite," the infinite of complexity, which is as real as
infinitesimalness and immensity. Consciousness presents itself experimentally as the *specific element* of this complexity pushed to extreme
values.

If the law of recurrence (called the law of complexity/conscious-
ness) is applied to the history of the world, one observes a growing
series of critical points and singular developments taking shape.[2]

[1] Since we should here cross our t's and dot our i's (the most recent
reviews of *Le phénomène humain* show that the crudest misinterpretations are
tirelessly repeated, and that in such matters we cannot sufficiently stress the
obvious distinctions that must be made), let us remember that Teilhard
placed himself on the plane of phenomenological analysis. He expressly left
a place open for an analysis of another, a metaphysical, order. Thus the law
of recurrence, according to which reflective consciousness *appears* when a
certain threshold of complexity has been reached, does not make the emergence of consciousness and a special creative intervention of God mutually
exclusive. On the contrary, the law of recurrence shows the manner in which
this creative action is realized.
[2] "Un sommaire de ma Weltanshauung," 1954.

What is complexity?

Teilhard has on many occasions very precisely defined what he understands by a growing "complexity." The definitions dealing with it are found in the texts which were written after *Le phénomène humain.*

By the complexity of a whole, Teilhard does not only understand the number and variety of elements forming this whole.[3] Further, by complexity, Teilhard does not straightway designate *simple aggregation*, that is, any assemblage whatsoever of non-arranged elements as, for example, a pile of sand.[4]

Assembled in ordered arrangement the 360 types of atomic nuclei of hydrogen and uranium known to modern physics constitute a heterogeneity, not a complexity.

In this sense a planet is heterogeneous and not complex. Complexity is an organized heterogeneity. Complexity is not the same as the simple indefinite geometric repetition of unities as seen in the phenomenon of crystallization.[5]

Thus by complexity Teilhard specifically understands a combination, or in his own words, as "that particular form of grouping, characterized mainly by the fact that it binds a certain fixed number of elements to itself — with or without the auxiliary contribution of aggregation or repetition — in a closed whole having a determined radius, for example the atom, the molecule, the cell, the metazoa, etc." [6]

In the case of aggregation or crystallization the arrangement, by nature, remains in a constant state of incompleteness, externally. A new contribution of matter is always possible. In a heavenly body, or in a crystal, there is not trace of a unity limited in relation to itself, but simply a system accidentally "contoured."

Through "combination," on the contrary, there appears a type of grouping structurally completed in itself at every instant.[7]

[3] "La place de l'homme dans l'univers, réflexions sur la complexité," 1942.
[4] "Le groupe zoologique humain."
[5] "La place de l'homme."
[6] "Le groupe zoologique humain."
[7] *Ibid.*

Complexity must be understood as that quality possessed by a being when that being is, firstly, formed by a greater number of elements, and in which, secondly, these elements are more closely organized among themselves. Thus an atom is more complex than an electron, a molecule more complex than an atom, and a living cell more complex than any chemical nucleus that might enter into its constitution.[8]

Complexity therefore is not determined only by the number and diversity of elements contained in the system, but also by the number and correlative variety woven between the elements.[9]

This concept of complexity "simply expresses a specific character for each species of body, as its mass, volume, or any other dimension." [10]

The yardstick of complexity permits us to establish a natural and genetic classification of the material realities which have appeared in the course of time.

This universal classification of natural unities can be expressed in a diagram. At the very bottom would be the 92 chemical elements, from hydrogen to uranium, formed by groupings of atomic nuclei, united with their electrons. Then would come molecules, formed by groupings of atoms. These molecules can in carbon compounds become enormous. Thousands of atoms are found linked in the albuminoids.

Above these on our diagram we shall place the viruses, and still higher, the primary cells. And at last we come to the world of higher living things in which each is formed by the grouping of cells.[11]

The advantage of this natural classification, essentially based on the inner structure of beings, is that it provides information on the historical genesis of beings. "On such a diagram, drawn up according to the order of complexity, the elements succeed one another *by historical order of birth*. The place occupied on

---

[8] "Vie et planètes," *Études* (May, 1946), p. 152.
[9] *Ibid.* and "La place de l'homme."
[10] "Vie et planètes," p. 153.
[11] *Ibid.*, pp. 153–157.

our table of complexities by each corpuscle chronologically locates this element in the genesis of the universe, i.e., in time. It dates it." [12]

To the extent that this natural classification exactly follows the contours of the real, and not only the curve of "complexification," it has the further advantage of grouping the corpuscular types, actually existing in the world under our eyes, in a way which our mind finds logically coherent. But in addition it expresses — and all modern taxonomy bears testimony to this — the manner in which they have been successively formed in the course of cosmic duration. [13]

Another advantage of the yardstick of complexity is that it liberates us from the ancient opposition between the sphere of physics and the sphere of biology.

No matter how great the difference in nature between life and matter which, it is believed, must somehow be maintained for philosophical reasons, a *law of recurrence* finally comes to light in the order of appearances, which experimentally connects the apparition of the two phenomena. Beyond a million atoms everything happens as if the material corpuscles become animated and vitalized, so that the universe arranges itself in a single grand series, doubtlessly more or less complicated, but on the whole clearly oriented in an upward direction, from the most simple atom to the highest living organisms. [14]

On the basis of a genetic point of view, to which we are brought by the law of growing complexity, "biology would be nothing else but the physics of this very great complex." [15]

What is the place of man in the universe? [16]

If one considers man, or only our planet in the universe from the spatial view of its vastness, we would appear to ourselves as lost between the "two infinities" of greatness and smallness.

[12] "Vie et planètes," p. 154.
[13] "Le groupe zoologique humain."
[14] "Vie et planètes," p. 154.
[15] "Le groupe zoologique humain."
[16] "La place de l'homme dans l'univers, réflexions sur la complexité," 1942, and in "Vie et planètes," 1946. The treatment of the subject, moreover, is identical in both.

"Upon reading the message of astronomy it might, at first sight, seem that the planets themselves are but a simply insignificant and negligible element in the world about us." [17]

"A gas of galaxies, and following upon it a gas of stars: this is truly an overwhelming spectacle (which to tell the truth we find impossible to picture to ourselves) in which our vision of the universe, directed toward immensity, culminates at the present time.[18]

"At first sight the planets appear not only like ugly daughters but, even worse, like strangers and intruders in the sidereal system; not only because of their small dimensions (they are dwarfs, even Jupiter if compared to the sun), not only because of the ridiculous feebleness of the energy they radiate, not only because of the brevity of their existence . . . but also, and this is much more serious, because of their mode of existence." [19]

But if instead of regarding the universe "from the geometric viewpoint of immensity," we shift to another plane and regard the same landscape this time from the bio-chemical angle of complexity without, of course, changing anything in its arrangement, what would we now see? [20]

A complete reversal of values, a reversal of perspective. Let us again place ourselves face to face with vast sidereal unities and solar galaxies and let us try to feel the weight of their importance no longer by the weight of their immensity, not even by the weight of their complexity (since nebulae and stars are aggregates), but by the weight of the complexity of the elements they shelter.[21]

If, despite their enormity and their splendor, the stars do not succeed in extending the genesis of matter much further than the series of atoms, in compensation, it is only on the very dark planets, and on them alone, that the mysterious ascent of the world toward higher complexes finds opportunities to continue.

[17] "Vie et planètes," p. 146.
[18] *Ibid.*, p. 146.
[19] *Ibid.*, p. 151.
[20] *Ibid.*, p. 152.
[21] *Ibid.*, p. 155.

No matter how imperceptible and accidental may be the place they occupy in the history of sidereal bodies, the planets, in the last analysis, are nothing less than the vital points of the universe. It is through them that the axis now passes, and it is upon them that the efforts of an evolution oriented principally toward the fabrication of great molecules henceforth concentrates.[22]

Thus man no longer appears to occupy the spatial center of the universe, as in the ancient naïve anthropocentrism, but he discovers himself really situated at the summit of time, at the point of an evolution oriented toward the highest complexes.

Is life nothing but a "mould" on the surface of matter, an inexplicable aberration in the universe, originating, as has been asserted, from the lack of antisepsis? Is life just an epiphenomenon? Does the reduced place that it occupies in the universe justify one in considering life as a negligible accident which occurred on a infinitesimal point in space?

In order to deal with this problem Teilhard found a point of comparison in the recent history of science: the discovery of radium. How was the new element to be understood. As an anomaly, an aberrant form of matter? Or, on the contrary, as a paroxysm? Was it a curiosity, or a new physics yet to be established?

Modern physics, Teilhard observed, would, of course, not have been born if physicists had stubbornly persisted in regarding radioactivity as an anomaly. Likewise, biology could not have developed and taken a coherent place in the scientific world unless life at last was recognized as the expression of the most significant and fundamental movement of the world around us. Despite its extraordinary properties, life, because it is so rare and minute in appearance, so localized on a sidereal particle and persists for so short a time, has been treated by physics (as was radium at first) as an exception and an irregularity, as an epiphenomenon.

Living matter for a long time has been regarded as an accidental singularity of terrestrial matter with the result that all of biology

[22] "Vie et planètes," p. 157.

hangs suspended from itself, so to speak, without any intelligible connection with the rest of physics. Everything changes, however, if for scientific experiment (as suggested by the curve of "corpusculization") life is viewed only as a specific effect (as *the* specific effect) of complexified matter: a property coextensive in itself with the whole of cosmic stuff but which is apprehensible by our vision only at that point where the complexity exceeds a certain critical value below which we see nothing.[23]

How mutilated our universe would be if we reduced it to the infinitely great and infinitely small — the two infinities of Pascal. "It is not simply on two, but on three infinities that the world is built spatially. There is no doubt an infinitesimalness and an immensity. But there is also the immensely complicated, rooted like immensity itself in the infinitesimal, but diverging later and following its own direction." [24]

After having for a long time been absorbed with the phenomenon of atomic disintegration, which tends to reduce matter to increasingly elementary and simple forms, physical chemistry henceforth is taking the reverse movement into consideration, namely the grouping of molecules among themselves which tends to lead to the formation of supermolecules more and more complicated.

With this perspective the science of matter rejoins the science of life. Corpuscles are animated by degrees of extreme physicochemical complexity, attaining combinations containing a million atoms. At the level of the virus the border between living and nonliving matter is blurred.[25]

Physics has above all concerned itself with following the phenomena in the direction along which they fall into a state in which they decompose and atomize themselves. The fact of evolution reminds us that the principal movement of the real is a synthesis in the course of which plurality is reduced to corpuscles of increasing complexity.

From a philosophical point of view this vision of things

[23] "Le groupe zoologique humain."
[24] *Ibid.*
[25] "Super-humanité," 1943.

liberates us from the ancient opposition between the One and the Many:

An indifferent and inert multiplicity does not exist in the bosom of complete duration. There are, without doubt, secondarily, dead ashes. But in itself, originally, dust in all its degrees is an index of nascent life. A first multiple is followed by first unification; at all the successive stages of consciousness, there is a new plurality which reconstitutes itself in order to permit a higher synthesis. This is how the law of recurrence in which we are caught up can be expressed.

There is no antinomy between the One and the Many if things are viewed as subsisting in a flux of personalization: they are simply just two phases (or more exactly two directions) of the same reality moving around us. Spirit and matter are contradictory only if they are isolated or symbolized in the form of abstract, fixed notions which are otherwise unrealizable, i.e., pure plurality and pure simplicity. In the nature of things the one is inseparable from the other; the one cannot be without the other. And this for the good reason that the one appears essentially as the consequent to synthesis of the other.[26]

We shall come upon this dialectic of the One and the Many again in the chapter devoted to Teilhard's metaphysics. Here we shall note only that while, in the order of the cosmos, an unintelligible dualism seems to impose itself inevitably between "matter" and "life," between matter and spirit, when they are inexplicably coupled together in a purely verbal manner, the relation between matter and life, between matter and consciousness, however, experimentally takes on a direction in the perspective opened to us by the disclosure of a cosmogenesis oriented toward the constitution of more and more complex syntheses.

There is no "materialism" here! "In the language of cosmogenesis, what specifically arrays the materialist against the spiritualist is *not at all* (as in a static philosophy) the positing of a passage between the physical infrastructure and the psychic superstructure of things, but *only* the placing, erroneously, of

[26] "Esquisse d'un univers personnel," 1936.

the *final* point of equilibrium of the cosmic movement on the side of the infrastructure, i.e., on the separated constituent.[27]

By discussing consciousness here we have anticipated the following chapter. But we shall see that, for Teilhard, consciousness, in a certain manner, is coextensive with life.

We conclude this chapter by indicating that, according to Teilhard, the increasing "complexification" is a cosmic drift comparable to gravitation in importance.

No longer is it a universal "attraction" gradually drawing the cosmic mass upon itself, but the power, still unperceived and unnamed, which forces matter (to the extent that it compresses under pressure) to dispose itself in corpuscles increasingly larger, differentiated and organized. Beyond and below, there is the *curve of assemblage* (gravity) and the *curve of arrangement* (complexity). There is no quiet drift toward equilibrium and rest, but instead an irresistible "vortex" churning the stuff of things, from the simple to the most complex, around itself in a one-way direction. And it churns into more voluminous and astronomically complicated nuclei. The result of this torsion in the arrangement of stuff is the rising, through interiorization, of consciousness (the psychic temperature) in the heart of the corpuscles successively engendered.[28]

[27] "Du cosmos à la cosmogénèse," 1951.
[28] "Le cœur de la matière," 1950.

CHAPTER 4

The Yardstick of Cephalization

The yardstick of growing complexity, which permitted us to read the direction of the cosmic process even as far as the appearance of life, from a certain moment onward, however, no longer suffices to help us in unraveling the direction of the, thenceforward, biological evolution of the world.

As long as one considers only relatively simple molecular unities, their order of complexity can be explained approximately by the number of atoms they contain. But, from the moment the number goes beyond a million atoms (as in the viruses) and, even more important, when we come to higher living unities, it becomes impossible to compute the number of atoms. Besides, as we have seen, this number by itself is not enough to determine the complexity of a corpuscle: Supposing that it can be determined, what remains to be evaluated is the number and the quality of the connections that have been woven between the atoms.[1] If the degree of organization of the super-corpuscles were as easy to measure as their length, there would be no difficulty. But as a matter of fact we know that, once we get beyond the molecules, the comprehension of the complexities escapes us by the very enormity of the values encountered.

How can we estimate the comparative complexities of a plant or a polyp, of an insect and a vertebrate, of a reptile and a mammal?[2]

Therefore we must find another and more precise yardstick in order to determine the direction of biological evolution.

[1] "Vie et planètes," p. 159.
[2] "Le groupe zoologique humain."

"Studied without any guiding thread it must be recognized that the host of living creatures qualitatively forms an inextricable labyrinth." [3]

Teilhard replies that what measures the degree of vitalization attained by matter at a given moment is its degree of "interiorization," its "psychic temperature," its level of consciousness.[4] What is the organ especially connected with the psychic development of being? Obviously, the nervous system. Here is the yardstick we were in need of to discover the direction of evolution in the inextricable diversity of secondary variations. We can now proclaim the *law of cephalization*.

No matter which animal group (vertebrate or anthropoid) whose evolution is being studied, in the course of time the nervous system grows in volume and arrangement and, simultaneously, it concentrates in the forward, the cephalic region of the body. Considered with respect to the details of their members and their skeletons the various organized types can be clearly differentiated, each one following a line peculiar to it, moving along the most diverse, or the most opposed, directions. Viewed in terms of the development of the cerebral ganglions life, all life, drifts more or less rapidly, but essentially like a single wave, rising higher and higher in the direction of larger brains.[5]

If in the tree of life we take that area of it which we know best because it is still full of vitality, namely the chordate branch, we see the emergence of a characteristic which paleontology brought to light a long time ago. We find the nervous system continually developing and concentrating, from layer to layer, by massive leaps.[6]

Among mammals the brain, on the average, is more voluminous and convoluted than it is among any other group of vertebrates.[7] "Among the infinite modalities in which the complication of life is dispersed, the differentiation of the nervous

[3] *Le phénomène humain*, p. 154.
[4] *Ibid*. and "Le groupe zoologique humain."
[5] "Super-humanité," 1943.
[6] *Le phénomène humain*, p. 136.
[7] *Ibid.*, p. 158.

tissue stands out, as theory allowed us to expect, as a significant transformation. It gives a direction, and by its results it proves that evolution has a direction." [8]

We cannot here go into the technical details of the facts and of their interpretation which warranted Teilhard to arrive at his conclusions. Let us content ourselves with the formulation of the two results obtained by the application of the yardstick of cephalization to the living world.

1) "The principal axis of cosmic involution (or of 'corpusculization') traverses the earth through the branch of the mammals."

2) "The terrestrial axis of corpusculization traverses through the order of primates, more precisely through the family of anthropoids." [9]

In this way the growing cephalization links itself to the growing complexity verified at the level of prelife.

Apparently life is nothing else but the privileged enlargement of a fundamental cosmic drift (as fundamental as entropy or gravity) which can be called "the law of complexity/consciousness," and which can be expressed as follows:

Left for a very long time to itself, under the prolonged and universal play of chance, matter manifests the property of arranging itself in groupings which are more and more complex and, at the same time, more and more enclosed in consciousness. Once begun, this double movement, coupled with cosmic involution (corpusculization) and psychic interiorization (or "centration"), is continued, accelerating and pushing itself forward as far as possible.

This drift of complexity/consciousness (leading to the formation of corpuscles more and more astronomically complicated) is easily recognizable from the atomic formations onward, and it asserts itself in the molecular structures. Evidently, it is but among living organisms that it is disclosed in all its clarity — and in all its additivity — at the same time as it changes into a convenient and simplified form: namely, *the drift of cerebration.*

In the growing perfection and cephalization of nervous systems it

[8] *Le phénomène humain*, p. 158.
[9] "Le groupe zoologique humain."

seems we veritably possess a concrete and precise yardstick which allows us to follow the absolute and useful variation of cosmic corpuscularity through the jungle of living forms.[10]

[10] "La structure phylétique du groupe humain," *Annales de paléontologie,* 37 (1951).

CHAPTER 5

Evolution Continues

This is one of Teilhard's major theses. We find it already expressed in one of his first writings, dated in 1916.[1]

Since the emergence of man, life, of course, has ceased to create new species. But evolution continues, along a new level and in accordance with new modalities, in the still uncompleted anthropogenesis. Anthropogenesis continues biogenesis which, in turn, had carried on the work of cosmogenesis. This is a scientific thesis of considerable importance to the philosopher; it signifies no less than that creation is continuing in man and with man. This is the constant teaching found in Holy Scripture, in St. John and St. Paul. Teilhard, on a scientific plane and at the level of appearances, shows us how the work of creation continues under our eyes through the genesis of man.

"Without doubt many biologists, and not the less important ones (all of whom for that matter are convinced that man, like everything else, has appeared evolutively, that is to say he was *born*, in nature), still hold that our species, by arriving at the stage of *sapiens*, is supposed to have attained a maximum organic limit. Henceforth, all it can do now is to establish a ceiling. Thus, for them anthropogenesis has no further interest except retrospectively, as a 'history completed.' " [2]

It is against this entirely gratuitous idea of an arrested "homi-

[1] "Even more than by organic transformations, evolution is actually continuing by improvements of a psychological order. It is the same ontological effort which is prolonging itself, but in a new phase, and on a new plane" ("La vie cosmique," 1916). Since then Teilhard has stressed the peculiarly biological aspect of the effects of the association of human elements upon themselves.

[2] "Le cœur du problème," 1949.

36

nization" that Teilhard endeavors to open our eyes to the evidence of a humanity in the full crisis of growth.

The laws with which the process of cosmogenesis, and then that of biogenesis, have been defined — association, the synthesis of elements oriented toward the constitution of corpuscles more and more complex, more and more vitalized and more conscious — this same law of complexity/consciousness continues to be verified at the level of anthropogenesis. But according to a new system, that of reflection.

Without any precise scientific reason but only because of the simple effect of impression and routine, we have acquired the habit of separating the *arrangements of individuals* and *the arrangements of cells* from one another as though they belonged to two different worlds. The latter alone have been considered as organic and natural, as opposed to the former which have been relegated to the domain of morality or artificiality. The social sphere, human sociality above all, is the concern of historians and jurists more than it is that of biologists.

Overcoming and disdaining this vulgar illusion, let us more simply try the opposite way. That is to say let us extend the above-mentioned perspective, valid for all known corpuscular groupings, from the atoms and molecules up to and including the cellular structures. In other words, let us decide that the multiple factors (ecological, physiological, psychic) actually at work in order to bring together and to link living beings in general (and more particularly human beings) stably among themselves are but the prolongation and expression, at this level, of forces of complexity/consciousness. And that they have been at work from the very beginning, let us say, to construct (as far as possible and it is everywhere possible in the universe) corpuscular ensembles of an ever-increasing higher order, in a direction opposite to that of entropy.[3]

Later on we shall consider this phenomenon of human socialization, which Teilhard views with the eye of a biologist. Here we shall note only that this human social phenomenon shows

[3] "La structure phylétique du groupe humain," *Annales de paléontologie*, 37 (1951).

that the evolution of life is not only not congealed or arrested on earth, but that it is embarking upon a new phase.

The active era of evolution (contrary to the commonly widespread or tacitly admitted opinion) did not come to a close with the appearance of the human zoological type. For by virtue of his individual access to reflection, man manifests the extraordinary property of totalizing himself collectively upon himself, thereby prolonging at a planetary level the essential vital process which, under certain conditions, leads matter to organize itself into elements which are more and more complicated physically and always more centered psychologically. Thus (and always, of course, on the condition that the organic nature of the social phenomenon be accepted) the network and the consciousness of a *Noosphere* — beyond any and all unity recognized or even theoretically foreseen up to now by biology — is about to weave itself around us.[4]

According to Teilhard, and Julian Huxley as well, man is still in his first infancy. Ahead of him, in the future, lies the promise of an adult state which Teilhard calls the "ultrahuman" in relation to the actually human. "Zoologically and psychologically speaking, man, when he is perceived in the cosmic integrity of his trajectory, is still only at an embryonic stage — beyond which a large fringe of the ultrahuman already silhouettes itself." [5]

Later we shall see how humanity will find its maturity in association. And in union. In this regard Teilhard employs expressions which cannot but recall the biblical conception of man in the specific sense of the term "adam," the *adam* who grows so that he may arrive at the stature of the plenitude of Christ. We are reminded, too, of the idea of the collective direction of a humanity called to a common and communal destiny found in St. Irenaeus, St. Augustine and Pascal.

Thus in the world around us there would not be only men multiplying in number, but there is still *man* being formed. Man, in other words, is not yet zoologically adult. Psychologically, he has not had

[4] "Le rebondissement humain de l'évolution," *Revue des questions scientifiques* (April, 1948), p. 166.
[5] "Le cœur de la matière," 1950.

his final say. But under one form or another, the ultrahuman is on the march; and this, as the result of direct or indirect socialization, cannot fail to appear on some tomorrow. Not only is it the unfolding future but a future which constructs itself before our very eyes. Here is a vision which, because he has begun to enjoy it in our own times, one can be very sure man will never again forget.[6]

[6] "Le cœur du problème," 1949.

CHAPTER 6

The Step Toward Reflection

After crossing the critical threshold of reflection, evolution entered a new phase and underwent a radical change. "Man is not only a new 'species' of animal, as some persist in repeating a little too often; he represents, he is the beginning of, a *new species of life.*" [1]

In science consciousness, like life, has often been considered as a subordinate phenomenon in the vast totality of things, as a bizarre exception, as an epiphenomenon without cosmic importance because it is localized in a tiny part of the universe. Vis-à-vis consciousness, Teilhard resumes the same argumentation he employed when he discussed gauging the importance of life in the universe. Just as physics was forced, in the presence of radium, so science must learn, when confronted by consciousness, to "discover the universal in the exceptional." [2] Teilhard's thought is that consciousness is coextensive with life. In this respect he is only taking up again an idea shared by Bergson and Le Roy.

According to Julian Huxley's definition, man is nothing else but evolution become conscious of itself. Man becomes aware of the ontological current which is sweeping him along and he takes over certain control levers. "Although it should not be thought that the organized mass forming the biosphere ever behaved in a purely passive way vis-à-vis the forces of vitalization, it does seem as if this mass, up to the time of the Pliocene epoch, was *led* rather than leading in the terrestrial history of

[1] "La réflexion de l'énergie," *Revue des questions scientifiques* (October, 1952), p. 485.
[2] *Le phénomène humain*, p. 52.

40

evolution. And for even a long time after the initial crisis of 'hominization' it seemed quite clear that the apparent direction of things had not sensibly changed." [3]

With man, evolution entered a radically new era: "After the era of evolutions passively undergone came the era of *auto-evolution*." [4]

However close man is, morphologically, to the great primates, among whom, in a systematic classification, he comprises but a simple "family," man is distinguished from all the other animals by the fact that he does not only *know*, but that he *knows that he knows*. "In him consciousness, for the first time on earth, turned in upon itself until it became thought." [5]

By this very means, by reflecting upon itself, life embarks on a new stage by re-enacting its previous phases, one by one — multiplication, compression, association, interiorization — but this time on a level of reflection. This is the meaning of the human phenomenon in the eyes of the scientist who views it as part of the total adventure of cosmogenesis.

The capital difference between this new phase and the stages already traversed is that the invention of life to a certain extent becomes identical with the invention of man. Man's creative work is nothing else, in the long run, than the lengthening and continuation of the work of cosmogenesis.

"Reflection, this psychological characteristic of a being who not only *knows* but *knows that he knows* — how much so we certainly don't realize sufficiently in our own minds — by the simple fact that it allows us to think about the world, to anticipate the future, and to direct our own evolution up to a certain point, by itself suffices to explain the sudden lead taken by the human being over all the rest of life." [6]

The laws of natural selection played the predominant role in the matter of morphogenesis and cerebration until the appari-

[3] "La structure phylétique . . . ," p. 72.
[4] "La réflexion de l'énergie," p. 483.
[5] "Réflexions sur l'ultra-humain," 1950.
[6] "La réflexions de l'énergie," p. 483.

tion of man. Since the advent of man the forces of reflective invention took the controls of evolution into their own hands.

Between the Pliocene animal world (so exuberant and open in the variety and distribution of its forms), and the human world which succeeded it (an astonishingly closed, structured world, dominating — or excluding — all other life), there is not only a difference in degree but a change in order (or, if one prefers, a change of condition). By its properties, its methods of invention, and its autonomy, the human *Noosphere* (however it itself may be rooted in the prehuman, as the prehuman is rooted in the preliving) represents, by all evidence, a *new* layer or shell, *sui generis,* appearing on the old biosphere.[7]

"The consciousness of each one of us is evolution perceiving itself and reflecting." [8]

As a result of this passage to the momentous state of reflection, evolution enters upon new conditions of existence. Until man, evolution proceeded with the self-reliance of a movement which owed nothing to the beings it begot along its course. But with man, evolution, in large measure, placed itself and its destiny in the hands of a creature. As a result, henceforth there are certain conditions to be fulfilled if the project begun is to be carried forward. For, from now on, man is capable of judging the process which carries him along, and upon which he is "embarked." But, what are the requisite conditions for man to consent to cooperate in this action which was undertaken long before him, but which cannot be brought to term without him?

Clearly, the phenomenology of evolution continues, once evolution has reached the level of man, under the form of a phenomenology of action. (Because of certain of its features, this phenomenology of action inevitably recalls that which Blondel elaborated on another, metaphysical, plane in his celebrated work of 1893.) The primary condition necessary in order that man may complete the work already begun is that evolution

[7] "La réflexion de l'énergie," p. 483.
[8] *Le phénomène humain*, p. 245.

(or, in metaphysical terms, creation) be revealed as having a *direction*.

Here, let us note in passing, lies the very great importance of Teilhard's work: it is concentrated precisely on the discovery of the direction of evolution in a positive manner. Modern man has a great need to be able to see this direction, if he is to escape a feeling of isolation and forlornness.

In man, evolution becomes automatically capable of forseeing its *future* at the very moment that it becomes both self-conscious and (at least axially) self-operating.

Far more important than the questions of structure (pattern) and process which until this point sufficed to cover the economy of nature, is the formidable question which now faces us: *impetus of evolution*. It is a biological problem of a new type which silently arises in our hearts and prepares itself to dominate us tomorrow, by means of the other and more general problem (which is also closing in on us): of finally constructing an energetics of man.[9]

The necessary condition which must be present so that humanity may consent to cooperate in the work of evolution is "for the world to be constructed in such a way that thought, which has evolutively issued from it, is warranted to judge itself irreversible in the essentialities of its conquests," [10] that is, that consciousness, which is the flower, as it were, of complexity, in one way or another must escape the decomposition from which, all things considered, nothing can preserve the corporal and planetary stock which bears it. From the moment that it thinks of itself, evolution will no longer be able either to accept or to prolong itself unless it recognize itself as *irreversible*, that is to say immortal.[11]

The question of direction appears linked to the question of time. The universe can have a direction only if the time which measures its genesis is irreversible and oriented toward a ter-

[9] "La réflexion de l'énergie," p. 493.
[10] "La structure phylétique du group humain," p. 76.
[11] "Le rebondissement humain de l'évolution et ses conséquences," *Revue des questions scientifique* (April, 1948), p. 178.

minus. In this respect a comparison between Teilhard's and Heidegger's thought suggests itself: Two visions of the world, two philosophies diametrically opposed to each other. The one, scientific, discovering the direction of cosmogenesis and the irreversible temporality of creation oriented toward a terminus of maturation; the other, scholastic and literary, affirming the essential absurdity of being. A philosophy of birth, of being-for-life, and a philosophy of being-for-death.

Teilhard criticized Marxism for likewise defrauding man of his future. According to Teilhard these philosophies precisely express the danger courted by an evolution-become-conscious-of-itself. The attention of biologists must be drawn to this peculiarity of the process of autoevolution that has already begun at the heart of the *Noosphere*; namely, external pressure gradually ceases to be effective, and only internal attractions can continue evolution. In other words, nothing can compel the evolution that has reached the level of man to continue unless the human element *itself wills it*. "I have often said, and I will repeat it: amid heaps of wheat, coal, iron, uranium — or under any other kind of demographic pressure — the man of tomorrow will go on strike if he ever loses the taste for the ultrahuman. And not just an ordinary taste for it, but a deep and violent one, a taste which constantly rises in him in concomitance with the growth of the power of vision and action. A taste, we might say, capable of becoming paroxysmal at the approach of the final paroxysm which he is charged to prepare." [12]

The irreversibility that is physically required in order that evolution be finally achieved is of a very special type. It means that the personal elements will not fall back into some primordial amorphousness; it means not only the conservation, but the fulfillment of the human person. "The law of the conservation of the personal expresses the fact that the rise of mind in the universe is an irreversible phenomenon. It asserts that the world will never come down again from any new height of consciousness which the mind has once achieved. Once life has appeared

[12] "La structure phylétique de group humain," p. 76.

in matter, the cosmos cannot thenceforward 'devitalize' itself. So also, once thought has been born of life, it is out of the question that life could ever retrogress to a prehuman level. Taken as a whole, consciousness can move forward, but not backward." [13]

"Conscious at one and the same time of his uniqueness and of the existence of a future, man perceives that, given the fact of his existence, it is impossible that there should be a destruction which would annihilate him completely, for it would mean the annihilation of a irreplaceable portion of the cosmic effort." [14]

Besides, what would be the meaning of "an irreversible and immortal" evolution if the personal elements engendered at the terminus of its effort did not attain immortality? "The irreversibility, thus disclosed and recognized, affects not just any part of our consciousness but its deepest, most precious and most incommunicable core. And this in such a way that the process of vitalization in which we are involved can be defined, at its limit toward the summit, in terms of 'ultrapersonalization' (this is true whether one envisages the totality of the system or considers just the destiny of each element in particular)." [15]

Let it be clearly noted that this is not a metaphysical demonstration of the immortality of the soul. We are not on the terrain of metaphysics, but on that of a "physical" phenomenological analysis. The study of physical reality teaches us that in order for the universe to be coherent it must be of an irreversible structure. In order "to save the phenomena" it must be admitted that the universe will not issue forth into nothingness.

This is a thesis already present in Teilhard's thought in 1916: "Would it be evidence of a faulty construction in the universe and would the world perish of an internal contradiction if it produced a mind capable of judging it?" [16]

How would a being react, in the presence of, and perceiving for the rest of his life, an end in which it appears that he must perish

[13] "L'énergie humaine," 1937.
[14] "La centrologie," 1944, no. 15.
[15] "Le rebondissement humain de l'évolution," p. 178.
[16] "La maîtrise du monde," 1916.

entirely? With resignation? With stoicism? Not at all, I would say. He would react with a legitimate revolt and desertion, unless this death holds out a form of, or a condition for, a new progress. To act is to create, and creation is forever. Therefore, reflective activity and a total disappearance that can be foreseen are cosmically incompatible. The association of thought and death in the same evolutive current consequently gives rise to a fundamental conflict which culminates in the destruction of one of the two terms in the confrontation.[17]

"Under pain of suffocating on itself, evolution, having become reflective, cannot be conceived as being carried out in a 'cyclical or closed universe.' Evolution is incompatible with the hypothesis of a total death." [18]

The universe presents itself to science as a phenomenon which for several billion years has been oriented in a well-determined direction. In order for it to continue its march, in order for it to consummate the enterprise launched (the plan of which is already readable by a study of the past), it is necessary that a desirable future be disclosed. Lacking this, the universe will appear like an immense travail, undertaken an immensity of time ago, only to miscarry in an absurd manner at the very moment that it approaches its terminus.

The scientist, familiar with the past march of the universe, will not hesitate to assert: "It seems that one point, at least, can be placed beyond all doubt by the *analysis of the present datum*, namely the growth of the mind must be held to be irreversible, unless one decides to admit that the cosmos is something intrinsically absurd. The mind, *in its entirety*, will never retrogress.

"In other words, in a universe of an evolutive nature the existence of mind excludes, by structure, the possibility of death in which the conquests of the mind would *totally* disappear, in which, to state it more exactly, they would no longer be preserved *by their flower*." [19]

[17] "L'énergie humaine," 1937.
[18] "La réflexion de l'énergie," p. 494.
[19] "L'esprit de la terre," 1931.

"Short of accepting the idea of a world destined to miscarry on itself because of a fault in construction, evolutive irreversibility and personalization (despite the anticipation of the future which they imply) are realities of a physical *not metaphysical* order, i.e., in the sense that, just like the dimensions of time and space, they represent certain general conditions which the totality of our experience must satisfy." [20]

The philosopher perhaps will object that Teilhard presupposes the very thing which is in question: namely, that the universe is not an absurd phenomenon. Some contemporary philosophies indeed make the very claim that reality is intrinsically devoid of meaning.

Let us repeat, however, that Teilhard does not take a metaphysical, but a scientific, "physical" point of view. It is here that the difference between a vision of the world informed by positive science and a "philosophy" of a literary type becomes apparent. The philosopher may very well say and write that after all reality perhaps is absurd "by construction." The scientist who, by personal and concrete contact, is familiar with this universe, explored moreover in its spatial dimensions as well as in its temporal depth, knows quite well that the hypothesis of the philosopher is purely verbal.

Teilhard, of course, because of his regard for scientific rigor, agrees to admit the coherence of the real as a postulate. If one wishes to assert the coherence of the totality of spatio-temporal phenomenon, it is necessary to admit the irreversibility of evolution oriented toward the mind. But the man of science knows very well that the hypothesis of the intrinsic absurdity of the universe is, from the viewpoint of an extended knowledge of cosmic history, a gratuitous hypothesis the demonstration of which reverts to those who pose it — in short a highly improbable hypothesis. The certainty which compels recognition from a scientist is that the world, in its totality, is a well-constructed machine which "runs." It is this certainty which authorizes Teilhard's "physical" reasoning, based on reality:

[20] "Le rebondissement humain de l'évolution," p. 179.

A universe which would continue to *act laboriously*, while consciously awaiting absolute death, would be a stupid universe, a monster of the mind, as much as to say a chimera. Now since, as a matter of fact, the world presents itself to us, *hic et nunc*, as an immense action, developing itself at all times with a powerful sureness, it doubtlessly is capable of indefinitely nourishing a taste for life in that which is born of it, a taste ever more critical, exacting and refined. The world bears within itself the guarantee of its final success. From the moment that it opens the door to thought, a universe can no longer be something temporary nor limited in its evolution. It must, by structure, emerge into the absolute.[21]

Let us repeat that Teilhard's demonstration is not unconditioned as is a metaphysical demonstration. It presupposes a postulate grounded in experience. It remains to be seen, however, of what value an "unconditioned" demonstration — which is not based on a scientific analysis of the real — actually is.

The infallibility of the world is without doubt one of the major, "axial" certitudes which have informed Teilhard's thought, a certitude afforded by his long and passionate attendance to the problems of matter and existence. Rarely has the history of thought proposed such a love of the universe and of creation to us. We would have to go back to the prophets of Israel to find so deep a love and understanding of creation. Again we quote from a text in which Teilhard summarized his conclusions:

"If the world, taken as a whole, is something infallible (first stage), and if, in other respects, it moves toward mind (second stage), then it must be capable of providing us with that which is partially required for the continuation of a similar movement. By this I mean an *unlimited horizon*. Without this, the world, being powerless to nourish the progress to which it gives rise, would find itself in the inadmissible situation of having to vanish in disgust each time that the consciousness born of it arrived at the age of reason." [22]

[21] "L'esprit de la terre," 1931.
[22] "Comment je crois," 1934. This is reminiscent of the Scholastic adage: "Desiderium naturae non potest esse inane."

Teilhard's cosmic optimism does not exclude an acute awareness of, we might call it an obsession with, the risks of failure
attendant upon an evolution become reflective and productive
of man. We might perhaps call Teilhard's optimism a "statistical" optimism. He does not deny that many of the human
elements among those that are swept into the work in process do
not participate in the movement and are simply lost. Nor does
he deny — rather he stresses — the manifest danger of an evolution now capable of denying or inverting itself. The risk of
failure came into the world with consciousness, with man. But
Teilhard assures us that as far as the world and the universe are
concerned everything has been foreseen and all the requisite
conditions have been fulfilled so that an evolution become reflective may consent to carry on the project undertaken and
embarked upon. If there is a failure the fault must be imputed
neither to the universe nor creation, but to man. In the philosophies of the absurd, Teilhard saw the disquieting signs of an
"ennui" which, for him, is the greatest and the only danger
which can menace evolution.

As for the rest, it is evident that in Teilhard there is that
"statistical" assurance of the final success of the universe which
he never doubted. This is a scientific assurance which actually
corresponds to the virtue of hope. Assuming and integrating the
risks of failure, Teilhard's optimism is, to use a phrase that
Emmanuel Mounier applied to Christianity itself, a tragic
optimism.

CHAPTER 7

The Convergence of Evolution

In principle, the Bergsonian vision of the world was formed in accordance with an attempt to be faithful both to experience and to a reality that had been scientifically explored. Thus the discovery of the positive value of time proceeds from a reflection on the biological fact of evolution. But the Bergsonian cosmogony is also completely laden with grand Plotinian intuitions which Bergson rediscovered in Spinoza. The course on Plotinus which Bergson gave at the Collège de France in 1912 testifies, if testimony were needed, to the affinity between his metaphysics and that of Plotinus. Bergson himself declared: "Every man has two philosophies, his own and Spinoza's."

"Inversion" plays a considerable role in the Bergsonian vision of the world. It is the slackening of the *élan vital*, the inversion of the creative movement which begets the spatiality of things, the multiplicity of beings, the incapacity of our intelligence to comprehend the direction in which creation is developing; for Bergson matter is the principle of individuation. One can, of course, find texts in which Bergson asserts that the tendency to differentiation is already present in the very first steps of the creative movement. But primarily, individualities are formed in the encounter with the movement of reversion — i.e., materiality. As with Aristotle individuation is attributed, in an ambiguous way, at one time to matter, at another to form. We are familiar with the criticisms that Laberthonnière leveled at Bergson on this score. Bergson corrected his thinking in his *The Two Sources of Morality and Religion*. But he still retains the idea that the terminus, the goal of creation seems to consist in the advent of "heroes" and "saints," whereas with Teilhard, as we shall see, the terminus of the creative work in progress is not a multiplicity of persons, but the unity of a mystical body, which remains respectful of the persons who constitute it.

With Bergson, as with Plotinus, the One is at the beginning and the Many proceeds by a movement which "conversion" would perhaps be able to reabsorb. Simplicity is always more true than multiplicity. Whereas with Teilhard the One — a unity of complexity and of synthesis — is at the terminus, the end of the creative process.

Bergsonian evolution diverges. Teilhardian evolution converges at the summit, and is oriented toward a personal and transcendental unity.

In his spiritual autobiography Teilhard tells us how this lack of convergence, in the Bergsonian vision of the world, prevents evolution from fulfilling itself.[1]

Thanks to his scientific and phenomenological method, Teilhard escaped the restrictions of Alexandrian "movement" in philosophy. Far from falling back into materiality, Teilhardian evolution converges rather at the top, drawn toward a summit of personalization and unification.

When we appeared at the beginning of the Quaternary Period, the group of primates to which we belonged still distinctly showed that tendency to diversify and divide into subfamilies that was so characteristic of all living groups which had preceded it. The fossil men of the Far East (Pithecanthropos, Peking Man, and the Solo Man) form, it seems, a veritable shell or scale that is independent and marginal, that betrays the fact that elsewhere there existed (in Asia and

[1] Teilhard gave evidence of his disagreement as early as 1917 (it is true that at that time Teilhard had read only *Creative Evolution*): "Whereas in Bergson's *Creative Evolution*, the cosmos is revealed as a widespread irradiation as from a spouting center, the shape of the universe as disclosed in the 'creative union' is that of a reduction or a leading back, of a convergence, of a centripetal confluence from some sphere infinitely distended. Equally evolutive, the two theories are the reverse of one another" ("L'union créatrice," 1917).

"By the sole fact that one recognizes the shape of a convergence in universal Becoming, the Bergsonian idea of a vital *thrust* without finality, of a *vis a tergo* is eliminated. In effect such a dynamism admits a center of divergence from the outset. One cannot see how it would produce the confluence of elements which it drives ahead of itself" (*Ibid.*).

Africa) other forms that were closer to the heart of the development, but were still so many scales. So, at birth, there was a "bulb" of the ruminants or carnivores. But soon, apart from this tendency to branch out, certain elements of union became manifest. By the end of the Paleolithic Age, the *sapiens* group (despite its own branching out — into white, yellow and black) formed a closed system. Thus a movement of withdrawal or of convergence appeared and asserted itself in the course of two successive phases (one expanding, the other compressing) in which lies the most essential characteristic of the human phenomenon, or so I believe.[2]

In its prehuman phase, biological evolution was characterized by a diversity and a branching-out. With man evolution withdraws upon itself to produce an inflorescence, as they say in biology, at the tip of the stem. "Like any other particle of living matter, the human 'species' basically tends to multiply itself to the maximum. But in contrast to what goes on in a school of fish or in a colony of bacteria, this multiplication, instead of simply increasing the number of the constituent members of the population, engenders in the whole of the group, a 'state of expansion,' a system of structures which are always linked to each other in a greater degree than they were before and they are always better centered." [3]

This is the way in which the great law of complexity and association, which we have seen at work at the lower stages, in cosmogenesis and biogenesis, is confirmed at the human and reflective level: "Under this rationalized form, even though its events are human ones, human history, according to its own way and method, does really prolong the organic movement of life. Though it may be speaking of social ramifications it is *still* natural history." [4] After gradually covering the earth with a living tissue that is loosely socialized, humanity is about to "join itself to itself racially, economically and mentally, and with a constantly accelerating speed and pressure. . . . Irre-

[2] "Comment je vois," 1948, no. 12.
[3] "La réflexion de l'énergie," p. 481.
[4] *Le phénomène humain*, p. 231.

sistibly, the human world is driven to unite. It is converging upon itself." [5] "With homo sapiens, under the cloak of socialization, the axial vitalizing of matter sets foot upon a new stage. No longer is it a question of just one individual reflecting upon himself, but of millions of human reflections which seek and strengthen each other." [6]

Let us imagine, says Teilhard, a pulsation normally entering a sphere at the south pole and going through to the north. Two phases can be distinguished in the movement of the wave: one, a phase of expansion (from the south pole to the equator), the other phase one of contraction (from the equator to the north pole). The two phases, developing equally in a curved environment, converge.

For about thirty thousand years, the convergent dispersion of homo sapiens was carried out in an open system (the phase of expansion). In contrast, for some time now we have been witnessing the manifestation of the second phase, the phase of contraction, or in Teilhard's words, "a coming of the entire human mass into general contact with itself, without any trace of a slackening in evolution." [7] Until the coming of man, life remained divided even though it covered the earth completely. It was a collection of a tufts of juxtaposed species more than a network, or a tissue of organized fibers. Everything changes with the emergence of thought: the *Noosphere* tends to constitute a real biological unity. Teilhard developed and illustrated this thesis abundantly in his final writings. This is not the place for an exhaustive treatment of his argumentation. Moreover the present work has not been designed to substitute for reading Teilhard himself. On the contrary, its aim is to introduce readers to his works and to help them by sorting out the essential stages of the dialectic which constitute the axis of this view of the world. Thus the reader is referred to the numerous articles published by Father Teilhard in recent years which have appeared

[5] "La réflexion de l'énergie," p. 481.
[6] "Le structure phylétique . . . ," p. 67.
[7] *Ibid.*

in the *Revue des questions scientifiques,* in the *Annales de paléontologie,* as well as in other publications.

Here we shall note only that the scientific thesis of the convergence of humanity upon itself, by which evolution draws to a close in a sort of inflorescence, is a very old idea in Teilhard's thought. True, it is expressed in terms that are more metaphysical than scientific in one of his first essays: "Socially speaking," wrote Teilhard in 1916, "the human monad presents itself to external or even closer observation as a sort of molecule or cell, essentially destined to be integrated in a higher structure or organism. Not only does it require the nourishment of the numerous material perceptions and assimilation indispensable to its constitution, but for its full development it requires the complement of other monads similar to it. *It can never absolutely be itself* except by ceasing to be alone." [8] The human monad, like a cell, needs to integrate itself into a body in which it finds fulfillment.

This same idea is found in the writings of his mature period, but this time in scientific dress. "In addition to being an individual centered in relation to himself, i.e., a 'person,' does not man also represent an *element* in relation to some new and higher synthesis? We know that atoms are the sums of nuclei and electrons, and molecules the sums of atoms, and cells the sums of molecules. Ahead of us then would there not be a humanity in the process of formation, the sum of organized persons? And for that matter isn't this the only logical way of prolonging, by *recurrence,* the course of universal 'moleculization,' in the direction of a centered complexity and a greater consciousness?" [9]

In his spiritual autobiography Teilhard wrote: "I can say, in this year of 1950, that the evolution of my interior vision culminates in this evidence of a 'creative' drift carrying along the human megamolecules, under the very statistical effects of their growing freedom, in the direction of an incredible 'quasi-mono-molecular' state in which, in conformity with the biologi-

[8] "La vie cosmique," 1916.
[9] "La place de l'homme dans l'univers," 1942.

cal laws of union, each *ego* is destined to attain its paroxysm in some mysterious superego." [10]

In this part of our presentation we shall confine ourselves to the plane of his scientific synthesis. In the chapter devoted to Father Teilhard's theological thought we shall see how this idea of a personalizing association of human elements is projected further within a Christian perspective.

Here we shall stress a thesis, an axiom which Teilhard tirelessly repeats over and over again, namely that *union differentiates*.

Because of our sense of individuality we are seized by a legitimate anxiety before the evidence of a convergence of humanity upon itself, and of a mass contact of humanity. Will not this totalization, as with termite nests, or totalitarian states, wipe out, or force the regression of, personality, so precious and obtained at such great cost? Teilhard's answer to this question is that totalitarian states represent aberrant or pathological forms accidentally assumed by the phenomena of socialization. But biologically they are not the essence of the phenomenon.

Let us observe any one of the unifications of *convergence* which take place in the field of our experience. For example, the grouping of cells in a living body, the grouping of individuals and functions in a social organism, the grouping of souls under the influence of a great love. We will then come to a factual conclusion which easily justifies our theory that the phenomena of fusion or dissolution in nature are but signs of a return to a diversity within a state of homogeneity. Union, real union toward the summit, within the mind, ends up producing the perfection peculiar to the elements that it dominates. Union differentiates.[11]

In any domain — whether we are dealing with the cells of a body, the members of a society, or the elements of a spiritual synthesis — *union differentiates*. In every organized whole the parts perfect and fulfill themselves. Because they neglected this universal rule, many a system of pantheism has misled us into the cult of a great All in which individuals were supposed to lose themselves like a drop of

[10] "Le cœur de la matière," 1950.
[11] "L'énergie humaine."

water in the ocean or dissolve like a grain of salt in the sea. Applied to the case of the summation of consciousness, the law of union rids us of this dangerous and recurrent illusion. No, by following the confluent lines of their centers, the grains of consciousness do not tend to lose their outlines and to blur. On the contrary, they accentuate the depth and incommunicability of their *ego*.[12]

Obviously, then, there could be no greater misinterpretation of Teilhard's thought than to accuse it of pantheism.

Teilhard's scientific vision of the world is the most authoritative and demonstrative refutation that has even been made of pantheistic metaphysics, provided, of course, that metaphysics is really willing to heed the lesson of reality. Pantheist metaphysics proposed a conception of time in which time appeared as an illusory, negative greatness which the philosopher's knowledge strove to abolish, as the sign of a fall for which it was necessary to make atonement, and as a vision of things in which the multiplicity of beings was presented equally as an illusion, or as the result of a precosmic defect. In this metaphysics, individuation was brought about by a matter regarded as evil, or by a materiality regarded as an inversion, a degradation of being. Wisdom, moreover, consisted in striving to reabsorb the illusion of the Many, in order to arrive by reminiscence at the recognition that in reality we are all a particle of the One, *pars divinae essentiae*. Wisdom, in short, is the return to the primal One.

The exact opposite of this is a metaphysics which would heed the lesson offered by reality which has revealed its evolutive character. Time is surely a factor of differentiation, but this differentiation has a positive value. It is the creator of individualities and values, and of diversity which did not pre-exist in any way. The multiplicity of beings engendered in the course of time is not an illusion or an evil that must be abolished, but the very fruit of an evolution which tends completely toward the constitution of beings more and more free and more and more conscious. "Cosmic evolution," as Teilhard says, "carries out a project of a personal nature." [13] Evolution is irreversible,

[12] *Le phénomène humain*, p. 291.
[13] "L'énergie humain."

it will never turn back; it will not undo what it has laboriously created. Contrary to the cyclic time of the pantheist mythologies, the time of the universe is oriented in an irreversible way. If, in the metaphysics of a pantheistic type, wisdom consists in going back, if the consistency of things is to be found only in the past, in former stages, in the primordial; on the contrary, the evolutive vision of things looks for consistency in the future, in the ultimate synthesis. As can be divined, a whole spirituality results from this reversal. Research takes the place of nostalgia.

"Contrary to the appearances still admitted by physics the Great Stability is not at the bottom — in the infra-elementary sphere — but at the top in the ultrasynthetic sphere." [14]

"If things hold and hold together, it is only by reason of complexity, *from above*." [15]

In his spiritual autobiography Teilhard relates how, after at first having been attracted by pantheist systems of an Indian and Spinozist type in his youth, the discovery of the real compelled him to reverse his perspective.

Leaping directly from the old static dualism which paralyzed me, in order to emerge in a universe not only in a state of evolution but of a *directed evolution*, i.e., of *genesis*, I was led to carry out a veritable "about-face" in the fundamental pursuit of consistency. Until then my directive sense of plenitude tended to orient and fix itself on the side of the extremely simple, i.e., of the physically indecomposable. Thenceforward, since for me the unique and precious essence of the universe had taken on an evolutive form in which matter is transformed into thought by means of the prolonged effect of *Noogenesis,* I found myself inevitably and paradoxically led to identify the extreme solidity of things with an extreme *organic complexity.*[16]

Teilhard has often said that the beginnings of a process are the least instructive, no matter how they may appeal to our curiosity. It is at the terminus of things that the direction and consistency of everything is to be found.

[14] *La phénomène humain*, p. 301.
[15] *Ibid.*, p. 37.
[16] "Le cœur de la matière."

CHAPTER 8

The Omega Point

The history of cosmogenesis and anthropogenesis thus presents itself as a continual effort at a synthesis tending to the constitution of corpuscles more and more complex, vitalized and conscious; at the termination of this process, in the future, appears a humanity joined to itself in a unity which is not only respectful of the differences between persons freely integrated, but which is also personalized through the contribution of the *other*, infinitely multiplied for each monad. An analysis of this phenomena discloses a summit of complexity and personalization.

Extended indefinitely backward along the axis of time, the law of centro-complexity allows us to glimpse zones increasingly diffused in which increasing fragmentized elements of consciousness float in an increasingly disorganized state of heterogeneity. On that side there is no lower limit to "recurrence." It is the lower layer of the cone which extends itself indefinitely. On the other hand, driven in an opposite direction, i.e., toward the future, the extrapolation of the series defines a *summit*. The existence of a cosmic Omega Point appeared to us, from the moment the evidence that the universe was physically convergent had imposed itself on our mind.[1]

To be sure, and this is something which Teilhard himself asserts, the elucidation of the Omega Point at the terminus of the spatio-temporal phenomena proceeds from an extrapolation. Many scientists who follow Teilhard in his analysis of growing complexity, of cephalization, of the convergence of evolution, do not accept this last stage of his vision of the world. The synthesis already presented is based on an analysis of the

[1] "La centrologie," 1944, no. 18.

past and the present. The elucidation of the center of the Omega convergence is a "view" projected into the future.

"For a very long time," writes Teilhard, "from the moment, in fact, when the equilibrium of the world, under my eyes, had been reversed from backward to forward, I never ceased to have a presentiment of the existence of a pole, not only of attraction but of *consolidation*, at the head of cosmogenesis, i.e., a pole of irreversibility." [2] "By structure the *Noosphere*, and more generally the world, represents a whole which is not only closed but also *centered*. Space-time is necessarily of a *convergent nature* because it contains and engenders consciousness. Consequently, its enormous layers, followed in the right direction, somewhere ahead must become involuted at a point — let us call it Omega — which fuses and consumes them integrally into itself." [3]

As regards the argumentation by means of which Teilhard sorts out the reasons for admitting the existence of a center of convergence lying ahead of us, we refer the reader to Teilhard's works themselves. It is not our intention, nor could it be, to substitute for the actual reading of Teilhard's texts. Our only aim is to facilitate this reading by offering a simplified schema of his endeavors.

Upon analysis the center of Omega convergence appears to mark a threshold of maturation of the whole cosmic process.

From the strictly phenomenal point of view we have adopted and adhered to, it seems to me that one can state the following:

We know that, at the very beginning, that which made man is the arrival of the individual consciousness at reflection.

In the course of the succeeding centuries, that which measures the progress of humanity is (as I have attempted to prove) an augmenting of this reflective power by the conjoined reflection of human consciousnesses among themselves.

Now, because of continuity and heterogeneity, that which will crown and limit collective humanity at the end of its evolution is,

[2] "Le cœur de la matière."
[3] *Le phénomène humain*, p. 288.

and can only be, a kind of pinpoint at the center of the reflecting apparatus taken in its totality.

Envisaged thus, human history would therefore develop entirely in the interval included between two critical points: a lower and elementary first point and a higher and *noospheric* second point of reflection. Biologically speaking humanity will not fulfill itself, and will not find its internal equilibrium (not before some millions of years perhaps) until it finds itself psychically centered upon itself.[4]

Humanity — that is to say reflective evolution — will not fulfill itself until it becomes organically one.

"In the system whose logic we have adopted, humanity is not yet the terminus of the cosmos because it is still multiple. This means that by the sole fact that evolution traverses the human person without stopping there, we are forced to postpone to some infinite future the terminus of the movement by which we are swept along." [5]

Bergsonian evolution, as we noted in the preceding chapter, fulfills itself through the flowering of "heroes" and "saints," i.e., through a multitude of "gods." (The universe as a machine for the fabrication of "gods.")

At its terminus Teilhard's vision is unitary. The end of the world can not be anything but the real unity of beings in the diversity of their persons.

What are the requisite conditions in order to make such a unification possible?

Here again we come across the dialectic which Teilhard has already employed to show that for evolution to fulfill itself it must appear as irreversible, i.e., immortal in the end.

In order to make the unification of human monads possible, the existence of a personal and already subsisting center of convergence, on which the monads graft themselves must be posited.

"Union differentiates. By virtue of this fundamental principle elementary personalities can, and can do nothing else but, affirm

---

[4] "Une interprétation plausible de l'histoire humaine: la formation de la Noosphère," *Revue des questions scientifiques*, 1947.
[5] "Esquisse d'un univers personnel."

themselves by coming to a higher psychic unity or soul. But only *on one condition*, namely that the higher center, to which they attach themselves *without mixing*, itself possess an autonomous reality. Since there is neither fusion nor dissolution of elementary persons, the center in which they all come together *must necessarily be distinct* from them, that is it must have its *own personality.*" [6]

From the moment evolution becomes conscious of itself, and reflective, the problem of action is posed for it out of physical necessity. At the human level a phenomenology of action, which analyzes its implications, demands and needs, must continue the phenomenology of evolution.

At the moment life reflects upon itself — and by virtue of this very action — it finds itself facing the *problem* of action. It awakens already on the difficult path of a progressive unification. How will this primordial, congenital obligation be justified? Where will life find, not only the legitimation, but also the courage and taste for this effort? . . . No consideration of any kind could rightfully authorize us to take the least step forward if we did not know that the rising road *leads to some summit* from which life will never again descend. Thus the only possible motivation of reflective life is an absolute, that is to say a divine, termination.[7]

From the moment that life becomes capable of judging and criticizing itself, our action is no longer possible unless life knows that its work represents a permanent acquisition. Now the best of our work is ourselves, our being, at the birth of which we are called upon to cooperate. No escape is possible in the presence of this principle, we shall not be satisfied by the hope that "our works" will serve posterity. It is our very own person that we would have immortal; lacking this, in the long or short run, we would go on strike, so to speak. "Two conditions are necessary, and in fact sufficient, in order to make us consent to, and cooperate with, the beckonings of evolution: the universal and superhuman terminus to which the latter is leading

[6] "L'énergie humaine."
[7] "L'esprit de la terre."

us must present itself to us simultaneously as *incorruptible* and *personal*." [8]

This center of convergence toward which all creation tends cannot be only an apparently real center. It must be subsistent and transcendent in order to be in a position to attract the thinking monads to itself. It is not the result of their convergence, on the contrary, it is the very cause and principle of convergence.

Under the penalty of being less evolved than the termini which its action animates, *universal energy must be a thinking energy*. Accordingly the attributes of cosmic value, which to our modern eyes it gives off, in no way remove the necessity on our part of recognizing in it a transcendent *form of personality*.

In no way can the definitive summit of the fulfilled, i.e., the personalized, world (namely God) be conceived as being wholly begotten by a sort of aggregation of elementary personalities (since by nature they must have a center). In order to *superanimate* a universe formed of personal elements, *without destroying it*, it itself must be a special center.[9]

This is not, let it again be clearly stressed, a metaphysical demonstration of the existence of God. As Msgr. Bruno de Solages has so properly stated in the text cited at the very beginning of our discussion, Teilhard leads us along a strictly *physical* plane to the recognition of a personal, transcendent Center, toward which creation converges, and in which it finds its consistency.

In order for the universe to fulfill itself and for the action in progress to arrive at its normal terminus, one must admit that the universe will eventually recognize before itself that *Someone* with whom it desires to unite.

All that remains is an escape-hatch, loophole solution which consists in the absurd assertion that the world will abort itself. Certain contemporary philosophies, indeed, do not at all hesitate to take this step.

But, as we have seen in the previous chapter, this thesis is

[8] "L'énergie humaine."
[9] "L'esprit de la terre."

more literary and emotional than positive. It is hardly possible except in the bosom of a reflection enclosed within a certain subjectivity which shuts its eyes on a universe in travail all around us. It is more a decision in favor of isolation and a cry of suicide, than a reflection on reality and Being, scientifically explored.

Clearly, Teilhard's vision of the world is opposed, point by point, to these despairing philosophies of existence. It is a cosmic philosophy, and it asserts that the universe can inspire hope if we but open our eyes, even slightly, upon it.

PART II

TEILHARD, CHRISTIAN THINKER

CHAPTER 9

Christology

From a theological point of view Teilhard de Chardin's work can be defined as an effort to shed light on the *natural* conditions and preparations leading to a *supernatural* consummation.

What Teilhard proposes — since modern science permits him to do so — is a *history of creation* as it has actually been realized historically, and as it continues to operate. Teilhard applied himself to disentangling a law of recurrence which experimentally defines the process of creation in the course of time. This law of recurrence is philosophically significant. It contains the great lesson that all creation appears as essentially oriented toward consciousness and personalization. Let us recall Teilhard's text: "Cosmic evolution carries on a work of a personal value."

At the terminus of this cosmic work of genesis, Teilhard glimpses a personal and transcendent center of convergence and consolidation.

All creation seems to be oriented toward a personalization centered upon a divine Person.

In his phenomenological analysis, Teilhard gives no name to this center of personalization; he designates it only, as is appropriate, by an algebraic letter, "Omega."

Until this point, we have remained on the plane of positive analysis and have limited ourselves to an inventory of the requirements that must be met in order for phenomena to achieve coherence.

In a further advance of thought, however, the Christian thinker is not forbidden to establish a relation between the lesson of reality and the lesson of the Word of God. Not only is this ultimate synthesis not illegitimate, but it is commanded by the entire biblical, patristic and theological tradition of Christian thought; in addition it answers an irrepressible need of the mind which cannot satisfy itself in the duality of some sort of inner partition separating the two sources of knowledge, creation and the Word of God.

Teilhard has been accused of "concordism" for having attempted this synthesis between the lesson of reality and the lesson of Revelation. "Concordism" is an illegitimate attempt to search Holy Scripture for knowledge which it is not meant to provide, knowledge which is ordinarily acquired by scientific investigation.

Father Teilhard's approach has nothing in common with concordism. To speak of concordism in his case is a lazy way of filing a new problem in an old pigeonhole. Father Teilhard's approach is not a searching of Scripture for scientific truths — he is quite far from that! — but a bringing together, within himself, of the sources of knowledge. And this the mind is inevitably led to do if it is to avoid having within itself artificial watertight partitions between truth and science. It is not a question of *confusing* the diverse sources of knowledge nor of mixing the principles and methods peculiar and specific to each order of research. It is simply a question of taking God's creation and the Word of God seriously. It is quite clear that our universe is the one of which Scripture speaks, and that there can be no contradiction between creation, which is the work of the Word of God, and this same Word expressed in human terms. Creation, in its physical, biological, human work, prepares that supernatural end to which Revelation invites us. And Christ Himself incites us to establish a parallel between the lesson of reality and His own word — to discern the *signs* of the fulfillment of His word in the real and in history.

"Now from the fig tree learn this parable. . . . When you see these things coming to pass, know that it is near, even at the door" (Mark 13:28).

Christian theology is not compatible with any kind of cosmology. The Stoic cosmology, for example, with its doctrine of eternal recurrence, or the Peripatetic cosmology, are radically incompatible with Christian theology.

Of this the Church fathers and the great medieval theologians were very much aware. And it was precisely in the name of the metaphysical — one might even say the "physical" — requirements of Christianity that they rejected the doctrine of eternal return, of the eternity of matter and of the divinity of the stars.

When, therefore, Teilhard tells us that a vision of the world in evolution makes a better symbiosis with Christian theology than does a static vision of the world, let us not be hasty in talking about "concordism." The issue here is not concordism, but coherence, and a coherence of a most elementary kind. The universe of a Plato, Aristotle, of a Chrysippus is incompatible with Christian Revelation. Thus there not only are the philosophical requirements of Christianity, but also the cosmological requirements of Christian theology. And that this is quite as it should be is clear if only one attends to the fact that it is the same God who created the world and who spoke to man.

The anticoncordist reaction — legitimate in itself — has engendered an aberration-in-reverse which may be formulated as follows: There is no intelligible relation between the real (creation such as it appears to us) and the Word of God, and this to such a degree that one might ask whether, indeed, it is the same God who is the author of the one and the other.

Instead of making a clear distinction between these domains, which is legitimate, the anticoncordist reaction has separated them. This makes the relations between the world and the Word of God unintelligible. The final outcome is an incoherent pluralism of "visions of the world": the biblical, the scientific, the philosophical and (why not?) the esthetic, etc. In the modern world the "homo biblicus" appears like a ghost. These remarks are made to forestall the criticism frequently leveled at Teilhard, i.e., that he confuses planes that should be kept separate and thereby revives the error of "concordism."

Teilhard has not built any watertight partitions in his mind between science and Christian reflection: therein lies his entire originality. He has viewed God's creation as sacred and capable of instructing us concerning the plan of the Creator. In this he stands in the most authentic, venerable, and constant biblical and Christian tradition, as it was formulated by St. Paul himself.

The whole of creation, St. Paul tells us, groans and travails together in the labor pains of birth, even until now. Teilhard's work is consecrated to the positive study of the cosmic, physical, biological, anthropological conditions which could concretely define this maturation of creation, through which it becomes capable of receiving the plenitude of its supernatural end. Far from confusing the order of nature and the order of supernature, Teilhard rather expressly reserves a place for the free gift of God, by attempting to describe the preparations with respect to this supernatural end on the part of the world.

When Christ invites us to discern the cosmic and historical signs which announce the end of the world, he establishes a relation between the physical state of the world and an event announced in a prophetic and supernatural manner. Thereby He testifies to the fact that it is indeed our world which is in question.

As a scientist Teilhard does nothing else but read these signs, in the history of the past and in the work of the present, which manifest an evolution of the world oriented toward a critical point of maturation.

"One can twist things around and around again as one pleases, still the universe cannot have two heads — it cannot be bicephalous." Consequently a supernatural process, which culminates finally in the synthesizing operation claimed for the Word Incarnate by dogma, will not take place apart from natural convergence of the world as it has been described above. There are, then, the Christocentrism fixed by theology, and the universal cosmic center postulated by anthropogenesis. All things considered, these two centers necessarily coincide (or at least overlap) in the historical setting in which we ourselves are

placed. Christ would not be the sole motive, the sole consummation of the universe were the universe, in some fashion, able to
cluster around something other than Him, even if it would be,
of course, at a lower stage. Christ, moreover, apparently would
have been physically unable to center the universe supernaturally on Himself, if He had not given through the Incarnation a
privileged point at which all the cosmic fibers tend to meet again
through their natural structure. Thus it is toward Christ that
we turn our eyes when, no matter how conjecturally, we look
toward a higher pole of human development and personalization. For us Christ, *hic et nunc,* both in position and function
occupies the place of the Omega Point." [1]

For the Incarnation to become possible it was necessary to
prepare a people and a woman, predisposed to this supernatural
visitation. Likewise in order for the world to fulfill itself in the
supernatural plenitude which is promised, and which all creation
awaits impatiently, certain conditions must be fulfilled: It is
necessary, if one can so express it, that creation, in its structure,
proceed ahead of Him who is coming.

Under the combined influence of science and philosophy, the
world more and more impresses itself upon our experience and
thought as a system linked together by an activity gradually rising
higher and higher toward freedom and consciousness. The only satisfying interpretation of this process is to regard it as irreversible and
convergent. Thus ahead of us lies a clearly defined *universal cosmic
center* to which everything leads and in which everything is self-
explanatory, conscious and self-controlled. In my opinion it is in this
physical pole of universal evolution that the plenitude of Christ will
be located and recognized. And this because *in no other kind of
cosmos* and *in no other place,* could a being, *no matter how divine,*
exercise that function of universal consolidation and universal anima-
tion which the Christian dogma ascribes to Jesus. In other words
Christ must be at the summit of the world if He is to consummate it,
just as He needed a Woman for His conception.[2]

[1] "Super-humanité . . . ," 1943.
[2] "Comment je crois," 1934.

The world is predisposed to its supernatural end. This, in short, in what Teilhard would have us perceive.

Too often the end of the world is presented under a form exclusively catastrophic. All of biblical thought, in fact, proposes the idea of a world in gestation which tends toward its fulfillment by means of a suffering which Scripture compares to the pains of parturition, and which is essentially fecund. The end of the world is the time of the birth of a new humanity, and a time of harvest. The catastrophic aspect, "the beginnings of sorrows" is but the negative side of this parturition. And, as is known, Scripture attaches an importance to the *duration* necessarily required for the fruit to ripen. In complete conformity with this perspective — and without, to be sure, having sought it out — Teilhard finds the direction of the preparations and of the "time" required for the coming of the end of the world:

Through habit we continue to think of the parousia (through which the kingdom of God on earth is to be consummated), and to imagine it as an event of a purely catastrophic nature, i.e., one capable of being brought about without having any precise relation to any determined state of humanity at no matter what moment in history. This is a point of view. But why not, in full conformity with the new scientific views of a humanity actually engaged in anthropogenesis (and in perfect analogy, let us add, with the mystery of the first Christmas which could not have taken place — everybody agrees on that — except between heaven and an earth that had been *prepared* socially, politically and psychologically to receive Jesus), why not admit rather that the parousian spark, out of a physical and organic necessity, can not be kindled except between a heaven and a humanity biologically arrived at a certain critical point of evolution, a particular degree of collective maturation? [3]

From the point of view of phenomena, Teilhard bids us observe the relation existing between "the critical point of human maturation, on the one hand, and on the other, *the point of parousia* (the second, triumphant coming of Christ) through which, at the end of time, the Christian horizon becomes fixed.

[3] "Le cœur du problème," 1949.

Inevitably, through their structure, the two points coincide —
in the sense that the attainment of the highest perfection of
humanity through ultrareflection appears like a prerequisite,
though not a sufficient, condition for its 'divinization.' " [4]

Never before, it seems, has a vision of the world — and a
scientific one to boot — been proposed as eschatological as
Teilhard's in both structure and essence. It is entirely oriented
toward the terminus and fulfillment, toward the coming of
Christ who "shall be All in All."

Throughout his entire life Teilhard had his eyes fixed upon
the resurrected Christ, toward whom all creation aspires, and in
whom it finds its consistency because, according to the expression of St. Paul, He is the Head of the Body, the Church.

From his first essay to his last writing, Teilhard never ceased
to assert the fullness of the cosmic significance of the great
Pauline texts and Epistles.

The Mystical Body of Christ is not only the juridical and
moral association of believers united around their Lord, in a
metaphorical way; the Body of Christ is truly an organism in
all the realism of this term, and in an eminent way.

For minds timid in their conceptions or imbued with indi-
vidualistic prejudices, who always seek to interpret the connections between beings as moral or logical relations, the Body of Christ
is apt to be conceived in terms of an analogy with human aggrega-
tions. Thus it appears much more like a social agglomeration than a
natural organism. Such minds dangerously weaken scriptural thought
and render it banal or incomprehensible to other minds excited by
the observation of cosmic physical connections and relations. The
Body of Christ must be understood boldly, such as it was envisaged
and loved by St. John, St. Paul and the church fathers. It forms a
new and natural world, an animated and moving Organism, in which
we are all united physically and biologically.[5]

From a theological point of view, of course, the use of words
like "natural," "physically" and "biologically" is not adequate.

[4] "Comment je vois," 1948, no. 24.
[5] "La vie cosmique," 1916.

But what matters to us in this youthful work of Teilhard's is to note the realism with which the Pauline texts are understood. Without diminishing Teilhard's thought, one perhaps could, on the contrary, express his intuition in a technically more satisfying manner by asserting that the Mystical Body is an organism — in a supereminent way and in a more real sense than all other known physical organisms, in accordance with its more stable and intimate connections.

Further in the same work, Teilhard repeats the assertion: "In truth the Mystical Body of Christ must be conceived in the manner of a physical reality — without any attenuation."

This Mystical Body is the People of God, it is the Church which is growing at this very moment. The fulfillment of the world is the plenitude of the Church of God. "The world is still being created and it is Christ who completes Himself in it." [6] Thus one can speak of a "Cosmic Body" of Christ.[7] Teilhard's "philosophy" in his first writings — and this is true of all his work — is the "philosophy of the universe conceived in accordance with the notion of the Mystical Body." [8]

Teilhard returns to these themes, again and again, throughout his entire life.

Despite the repeated assertions of St. Paul and the Greek fathers, the universal power of Christ over creation until now has been considered under an extrinsic and juridical aspect by theologians. . . . All the improbabilities vanish, and the boldest assertions of St. Paul take on without difficulty a literal meaning the instant in which the world, through its conscious side, is disclosed as suspended from the Omega focal point where Christ, by virtue of His Incarnation, appears, invested precisely with the functions of Omega.

If Christ thus occupies the position of Omega in the heaven of our universe (something which is possible, since Omega through its structure is of a superpersonal nature), an entire series of remarkable properties endow His resurrected humanity.

Physically and literally, first of all, *He is the One who fulfills*:

[6] "La vie cosmique," 1916.
[7] *Ibid.*
[8] "L'union créatrice," 1917.

there is no element whatsoever in the world, at no instant in the history of the world, which is not moved, which does not move itself, and which can never move itself, apart from His directive influence Space and duration are full of Him.

Physically and literally, still, He is the *One who consummates Himself*. Since the plenitude of the world will not be realized until the final synthesis, at which time a supreme consciousness will appear on the total complexity organized to the highest degree, and since Christ is the organic principle of this harmonization, the whole universe *ipso facto* finds itself marked by His character, planned by His choice, and animated by His form.

Physically and literally, finally, since all the lines of the world converge in Him and weave themselves together, it is He who gives its *consistency* to the entire structure of matter and mind. Accordingly it is in Him "the Head of Creation" that the fundamental process of cephalization fulfills itself and culminates, in universal dimensions, at supernatural depths and in perfect harmony with the past.[9]

All creation, St. John tells us, is made in the Word. It is also through Him that it will be consummated and then "God shall be All in All."

That the structure of creation be adapted to the fulfillment toward which it tends is quite as it should be. A universe of any kind whatsoever would not be adequate to this consummation *in Christo Jesu*. The universe as it was imagined by the ancients — a vast clock eternally turning around upon itself — is not "compossible" with the biblical and Christian vision of a creation which, during the entire duration of its genesis, tends toward its fulfillment in Christ.

If the world were a static cosmos — or further if it formed a "centrifugal" system — only (let us pay careful attention here) relations of a conceptual and juridical nature could be invoked to establish the primacy of Christ over creation. Christ would be the King of all things because He had been *declared* such, and not at all because any organic relation of dependency exists (nor could it even properly exist) between Him and a fundamentally irreducible Multiplicity.

[9] "Super-humanité . . ."

In this extrinsicist perspective one can hardly still talk honestly of a "Christic cosmicity."

But if, on the other hand — as has been established by the facts — our universe forms a kind of biological "vortex" dynamically centered upon itself, then how can we fail to see that a unique, singular position is disclosed at the spatial-temporal summit of the system where Christ, without deformation or effort, literally, and with unparalleled realism becomes the *Pantocrator*.[10]

What holds us back and prevents us from adhering fully to this idea of a creation really and physically fulfilling itself in Christ is the secret Manichaeanism that make us always forget that "all things were made by him" (John 1:3).

At first sight it might perhaps seem that it is difficult to reconcile this cosmic Christ with the evangelical Christ, Jesus of Nazareth, born of a woman and who died under Pontius Pilate. This is a question posed by any mind awakened to the discovery of an immensely enlarged universe. "Is the evangelical Christ, as imagined and loved within the dimensions of the Mediterranean world, still capable of covering over, and acting as the center of our prodigiously enlarged universe?" [11] Will not the sense of the cosmic Christ harm our sense of the historically incarnated Christ, *hic et nunc*?

Far from it!

Historically the cosmic Christ and the Incarnate Christ have always been conceived jointly by Christian tradition. And it could not be otherwise. "By virtue of the characteristics which at first would seem to particularize Him too much, *a historically Incarnated God*, on the contrary, is the only one who can satisfy, not only the inflexible rules of a universe in which nothing is produced or appears save *by way of birth*, but also the irrepressible aspirations of our spirit." [12] Teilhard is as far as one can be from Docetism.

The Church, like everything else, came into being historically.

[10] "Le Christique," 1955 — one of Teilhard's last writings.
[11] *Le milieu divin*, 1927.
[12] "Le cœur de la matière," 1950.

From the phenomenal and the "naturalist" point of view, the Church appears like a new "phylum" at the heart of creation:

> Considered objectively, by virtue of the phenomenon of the Christian movement, in terms of its roots in the past and its continual development, the Church exhibits the characteristics of a phylum.
>
> Reset in a context of an evolution interpreted as a gradual ascent of consciousness, this phylum, through its trend toward a synthesis based on love, progresses exactly in the same direction presumed for the leading-shaft of biogenesis.
>
> In the impulse which guides and sustains its advance, this rising shaft implies essentially the *consciousness* of finding itself in actual relationship with a spiritual and transcendent pole of universal convergence.[13]

Teilhard had a sense of realism about the Church which harmonized with his thought as a whole. The Church is the supernatural phylum planted at the heart of the *Noosphere*. For a person to leave the Church would make as little sense as for living matter to leave the phylum from which it receives its sap and life. Here again Teilhard is at the antipode of any Docetism or Calvinism. In the last analysis the axis of all creation passes through the Church.

We have first of all recognized that life is the central phenomenon in the universe, thought the central phenomenon in life and, finally, that the collective arrangement of all thoughts upon themselves is the central phenomenon of thought itself. Now by virtue of a *fourth option*, we find ourselves being led to decide that at a deeper level, i.e., at the very heart of the social phenomenon, a kind of *ultrasocialization* is in progress. An ultrasocialization by which "the Church" is formed little by little, and by her influence vivifying and bringing together the spiritual energies of the *Noosphere* in their most sublime form. The Church, as the portion of the world reflexively made Christ, the Church as the principal center of interhuman affinities through supercharity, the Church as the central axis of universal convergence, is the precise point of the encounter between the universe and the Omega Point.[14]

[13] *Le phénomène humain*, p. 332.
[14] "Comment je vois," no. 24.

CHAPTER 10

Spirituality

Teilhard's spirituality is the correlative to his vision of the world. As was stated at the beginning of this book, Teilhard is a twentieth-century mystic who knew how to let his positive, scientific knowledge of the world, and his understanding of the mystery of Christ grow correlatively within himself. In this respect Teilhard's attitude is profoundly biblical. His view of creation is biblical: Heaven and earth teach the glory of God, God can be known by the intelligence that studies His work. In Teilhard the love of creation developed at the same time as his love for Christ. Teilhard had hardly any training as a biblical scholar, but for this very reason the convergence of views is even more striking. Teilhard has spontaneously discovered the principles of a mysticism of the biblical type.

One experience was decisive for the genesis of Teilhard's thought. This was the schism between the best aspirations, the most legitimate demands of the modern world, and Christianity *as it was, and is still too often, presented.* Teilhard sharply resented, and in turn gave voice to his resentment, that diseased condition of Christendom, and of Christian spirituality which Nietzsche, Marx, and Freud — to cite only the greater names — so vigorously and so usefully denounced.

Teilhard de Chardin's spirituality can be defined as a magisterial effort to liberate Christian spirituality and mysticism from the residues of Manichaeanism which still secretly encumber it. Heresy is the sickness of Christianity. Manichaeanism is a sickness, a neurosis of spirituality.

We find a passionate expression of this decisive experience of being torn apart in Father Teilhard's first writings:

For after all must one renounce being human in the broad and deep sense of the word, bitterly and passionately human, in order to be a Christian? Must we, in order to follow Jesus and to participate in His celestial body, renounce the hope that we are getting the feel of and preparing a little bit of the Absolute each time when, under the blows of our labor, a little more of determinism is mastered, a little more truth is achieved, a little more progress realized? Must one, in order to be united with Christ, keep himself disinterested concerning the progress *peculiar to this Cosmos?*

At once so intoxicating and cruel, this progress carries us along with it and comes to light in the consciousness of each one of us. Does not such a process risk making mutilated, tepid, and weak personalities of those who apply it on themselves? This is the existential problem in the heart of a Christian where the divine faith which supports all human effort, and the terrestrial passion, which is its sap, inevitably collide.

It is my fondest conviction that any kind of disinterestedness about that which constitutes the most noble charm and interest of our natural life is not the basis of our supernatural growth.[1]

In his spiritual autobiography Teilhard tells of the conflict he himself experienced between the best of his human aspirations and a certain spirituality of flight and escape:

I find the first traces of this opposition during my years at secondary school in my pathetic effort to reconcile my interest in nature with the evangelism (certainly too narrow) of *limitation* whose texts nourished my morning prayers. Later as a scholastic at Jersey, I seriously considered a total renunciation of mineralogy, about which I was then very enthusiastic, in order to consecrate myself to the activities called "supernatural." If I didn't "derail" then it was because of the robust good sense of P. T. (master of novices). In fact P. T., under the circumstances, limited himself to telling me that the God of the Cross awaited the "natural" expansion of my being as well as its sanctification — without explaining how, or

[1] "La vie cosmique," 1916.

why. But it was enough to leave the two ends of the thread in my hands. And I found myself saved from the troublesome question.[2]

What Teilhard, with a very sure instinct, had turned down from the very start was a Christianity exclusively juridical, moral, individualist and Platonizing.

"Christianity," wrote Teilhard in 1916, "is a cosmic religion," [3] a "cosmogony." "Who then will be, finally, the ideal Christian, the Christian at once new and old, who will solve the problem of vital equilibrium in his soul by letting all the sap of the world flow into his effort toward the divine Trinity?" [4]

Certain of Teilhard's pages, in a sense, recall the *Confessions* of St. Augustine. In them we can see Teilhard making a heroic effort to free himself from this secret Manichaeanism which haunted the milieu in which he learned to know Christianity. "And this was to speak properly, the history of a conversion." [5]

I offer these pages in which I wish to present the best of my views of things, the loyal solution through which my inner life has found its equilibrium and unity, to those who distrust Jesus because they suspect Him, as they see it, of stripping the irrevocably loved face of the earth of its bloom and freshness; to those also who, in order to love Jesus, compel themselves to ignore that with which their souls are overflowing; and, finally, to those who, upon failing to reconcile the God of their faith and the God of their most ennobling work, grow weary and become impatient with a life split into oblique efforts.[6]

In these pages one already finds the themes that were to constitute *Le milieu divin* (1927).

The tragic thing about Teilhard's destiny is that he did not know how to situate and define, in a historical framework, for his own eyes and for those of his followers, this Christianity he had discovered; for it was simply the Christianity of the very

[2] "Le cœur de la matière," 1950.
[3] "La vie cosmique."
[4] "La maîtrise du monde," 1916.
[5] *Ibid.*
[6] "La vie cosmique."

beginning, of Scripture, of the fathers, and of the most constant tradition of the Church. This is the point at which one regrets all the more that Teilhard did not receive a theological training that emphasized the biblical and patristic sources. Teilhard spent his life fighting against a certain metaphysics, a certain theology, and a certain spirituality which do not correspond with anything real or essential in the Church; he fought an ensemble of misunderstandings, a phenomenon of triviality that too frequently, despite any effort, can take over an academic discipline; he fought against the sociological phenomenon of the perversion of Christian spirituality, with and against a sickness of Christendom.

Teilhard had the missionary's experience of the demands of the modern world in the matter of spreading the Gospel.

The originality of my belief is that it has its roots in two domains of life habitually considered antagonistic. By education and intellectual training I belong to the children of heaven. But by temperament and through my professional studies I am a child of the earth. Placed thus by life at the heart of two worlds whose theory, language and feelings I know, because of intimate experience, I have not erected any inner partition in my mind. But I have allowed two apparently contradictory influences to react in complete freedom upon each other in the depths of myself. Now at the end of this process, after thirty years dedicated to the pursuit of an inner unity, I have the impression that a synthesis has taken place naturally between these two currents which had been making contrary demands upon me. The one has not killed the other. Today I probably believe in God more than ever before — and certainly I believe more than ever in the world.

Is there not in this the particular solution (roughly sketched and on an individual scale to be sure) of the great spiritual problem which the vanguard of mankind is running into at the present time? [7]

Teilhard experienced the world of science and research as the missionary experiences China, Africa, or de-Christianized proletarian milieus. He learned its language, understood its legitimate

[7] "Comment je crois."

aspirations, and admired the human values exhibited in this world. Even his work is a testimony.

A testimony of my life — a testimony about which I would be all the less able to keep silent as I am one of those rare persons able to give it: For more than fifty years it has been my fate (and good luck) to be able to live in close and intimate professional contact — in Europe, Asia and in America — with all that which in these countries was reckoned, or is still reckoned to be, most significant, most influential and, one might say, most "general" with regard to the human substance. Thanks to these unexpected and exceptional contacts which permitted me, a Jesuit (that is to say one brought up in the very heart of the Church), to have access to, and to move around familiarly in, the most active areas of thought and free research, it was quite natural that certain things, to which those who have lived in only one of the two worlds are but slightly sensible, appeared to me with an evidence so compelling that they forced me to cry out.[8]

Nowadays the Christianity of the Christian appears, to the best among the Gentiles, like an undesirable mysticism, because it is underhumanized, morbid. On this point, of course, a rectification has been taking place on the Christian side for the past fifty years. The criticisms of Nietzsche, Marx and Freud have become less and less justified. But they were most likely not useless since they probably provoked this healthy reaction. One can also say that Father Teilhard de Chardin's action on behalf of the world is an important contribution to the healing process now taking place. . . . Teilhard, however, experienced the schism between the modern world and the Church at its most serious moment, i.e., at the end of the nineteenth and the beginning of the present century. "Indubitably, and for an obscure reason, in our time something just 'doesn't seem to go anymore' between man and the God who is *presented to the man of today*. Nowadays everything transpires as if man did not have accurately before him the face of the God he wishes to adore. On the

---

[8] "Le cœur du problème."

whole this is the source (despite certain decisive symptoms, which are still almost underground, of a renaissance) of that obsessing impression, all around us, of an irresistibly mounting atheism — or still more specifically — of a mounting and irresistible de-Christianization." [9]

One should not be overly hasty in blaming the Gentiles for their rejection of the Christianity that is presented to them. Rather, following the example of the prophets of Israel, what is necessary is to look for the sins and deviations within the people of God which explain this hostility to the Israel of God.

The vision of the world which imposed itself on Teilhard, the eminent scientist, naturally involves a renewal of spirituality. Man is not a being who has "tumbled into the world," or one thrown into an evil and absurd cosmos. Man, at the summit of cosmogenesis is called upon to cooperate with God who does not wish to fulfill Himself, as it were, without man's cooperation. "In its classic form," Teilhard writes

[and by that must be understood the training he received in school], the theory of Christian perfection rests upon the idea that nature (in contrast to supernature) in the actual world is complete — *fulfilled*. Numerically, of course, spirit still grows on earth (the multiplication of souls). But qualitatively (in its natural "powers") it spreads out and is going nowhere. It holds on, it simply endures. Under these conditions perfection for men can consist only in taking flight individually in the supernatural. The rest is of no interest to the kingdom of God, save to the extent that it assures, for an arbitrary period, the conservation of life through the ages. The children of the world largely suffice for this latter task. Essentially the Christian is more purely a Christian the sooner he detaches himself from the world. The less he uses creatures, the more he approaches the Spirit.[10]

One cannot deny that Teilhard gives a faithful description of this caricature which is sometimes taught, and, in any case, often

[9] *Ibid.*
[10] "Note sur la notion de perfection chrétienne," 1942.

understood, under the name of Christianity. One can recognize here the Catharist heresy, in a larval form, which so many Christians and nonbelievers confuse with the doctrine of Christ.

Thus Teilhard has only been fighting against a caricature. But this caricature, alas, is very real and it is a heresy. St. Irenaeus also struggled against a caricature of Christianity throughout his life.

Rediscovering biblical thought, without being aware of having done so, Teilhard, in opposition to this morbid presentation of Christian doctrine, asserts that creation is still in full gestation and that the duty of the Christian is to cooperate with it. "We are about to discover that 'the natural and supernaturalizable powers' of man are *still in full growth*, and this will probably be so for several million years still. We thought humanity ripe. As a matter of fact it is very far from being fully created, neither in its individual developments nor, above all, in the *collective terminus* toward which it is directed by virtue of the great phenomenon of the 'convergence of the Spirit.'"[11] By virtue of the creation still in progress, *continued* still, the kingdom of God appears as directly interested in the natural progress of the world; and the Christian, as such, accordingly finds himself obliged to cooperate in the fulfillment of the world so that it may offer an increasingly richer nourishment to the supernaturalizing process.[12] "Without deviating toward any naturalism or Pelegianism, the faithful person discovers that he can and must, even *more* than the unbeliever, conceive a passion for the progress of the earth, the requisite for the consummation of the kingdom of God. *Homo sum. Plus et ego.* And yet the upward-mounting force of detachment remains intact."[13]

Asceticism, consequently, no longer consists so much in liberating and purifying oneself from "matter" — as in the problematic of a Manichaean type — but in further spiritualizing matter, in unifying the Many, in participating in the consecra-

[11] "Note sur la perfection chrétienne."
[12] *Ibid.*
[13] *Ibid.*

tion of the world, in sanctifying and supernaturalizing the real which has been given to us, by "working together" with God, according to the expression of St. Paul. In the Christian perspective asceticism takes on an exalted meaning: it is a method of life.

The history of the world presents itself as a vast cosmogenesis in the course of which all the fibers of the real converge, without tangling, in a Christ who is at once personal and universal. Strictly speaking and without metaphor, the Christian who at one and the same time understands the essence of his Credo and the spatio-temporal connections of nature, finds himself in the happy situation of being able, through the whole variety of his activities, and in union with the multitude of other men, to enter into a unique movement of communion. Whether he lives or dies, *by* his life or *by* his death, he in some way consummates his God at the same time that he is dominated by Him. In short, in a manner perfectly comparable to the Omega Point foreseen by our theory, Christ, provided that He is disclosed in the full realism of His Incarnation, *tends to produce exactly* the spiritual totalization to which we looked forward.[14]

As is shown in *Le milieu divin*, not only are our activities capable of cooperating in the construction of the coming Jerusalem, but our very passivity, our failures, are retrievable and usable for the work of God by virtue of the efficacious mystery of the Cross:

From the point of view of convergent evolution to which sixty years of experience and reflection have led me, the whole cosmic event essentially leads back to a single and vast process of arrangement the mechanism of which (utilization of the effects of great numbers and the play of chance), at every instant, and for reasons of statistical necessity, releases a certain quantity of sufferings (failures, putrefactions, deaths . . .). Now it is precisely *the two facets* (constructive and destructive) of this operation which are penetrated and overcome by a wave of unitive power, through the accession of Christ to the Omega Point. Personalized in a single stroke and at the same time retaining all its developments which *center us for Christ,* cosmogenesis, even including its most implacable

[14] "L'énergie humaine."

and obscure determinisms, abruptly assumes the shape of innumerable contacts with a supreme pole of attraction and completion. A suddenly launched current of love spreads over the entire surface and the depth of the world. And this is not done only in the manner of some superadded heat or perfume, but as a basic essence destined to metamorphize, assimilate and replace everything.[15]

The Christian has the duty of being himself a creator, in some measure. Asceticism inevitably flows from this requirement of creation, for all creation, by its very essence, is painful, mortifying and crucifying. The mystery of the Cross is present, operating in all creation, in the whole of creation. "In action . . . I adhere to the creative power of God, I coincide with it; I not only become its instrument but its living prolongation. And since there is nothing more intimate in a being than his will, I merge it in some way, through my heart, with the very heart of God. This contact is perpetual, because I am always acting. At the same time, since I would be unable to find a limit to the perfection of my fidelity, or to the fervor of my intention, it permits me to indefinitely assimilate myself to God ever more closely." [16] "By virtue of the creation and still more of the Incarnation, *nothing is profane* here below on earth to him who knows how to see. On the contrary, everything is sacred for him who in every creature distinguishes the particle of the elected being that is subjected to the attraction of Christ in the process of consummation." [17]

Here can be recognized the celebrated texts of St. Paul: ". . . nothing is of itself unclean, but to him who regards anything as unclean, to him it is unclean . . ." and "for the clean all things are clean, but for the defiled and the unbelieving nothing is clean." [18]

Teilhard repeats with St. Paul: whether you eat or drink, do it in Christ Jesus.

[15] "Le cœur de la matière."
[16] *Le milieu divin*, 1927. -
[17] *Ibid.*
[18] Rom. 14:14; Titus 1:15.

In proportion as the world makes itself and creation is further elaborated, each epoch requires a new type of sanctity. And in each epoch sanctity, too, must be reinvented. Not only must each one of us, in obedience and fidelity to the motions of the Spirit, find his personal way to sanctity, but each epoch entails new requirements for sanctity. We cannot satisfy ourselves by imitating the manner with which this or that great saint of the past found his spiritual flowering. We must also produce a work of originality and creativity in the matter of sanctity. The principles remain the same, but the germ must be developed. This is what Teilhard tells us: "At the present time, what is lacking to all of us, more or less, is a new formulation of sanctity." [19] Throughout his life Teilhard applied himself faithfully to obeying his proper vocation which seems precisely to have been that of discovering, like a pioneer, a new type of sanctity, a new spirituality. As we said at the beginning of this chapter, this adventure, which Teilhard risked, led him to holy ground; Teilhard's spirituality lies exactly in its prolongation of biblical spirituality. What a pity that he did not know more about this biblical tradition the thread of which he resumed, without being greatly aware of the step he was taking. Thereby many misunderstandings and tribulations might have been avoided.

Even to this day I experience the hazards encountered by one who, because of an inner law and necessity, sees himself led to stray from the well-traveled, but now subhumanized, path of a certain traditional asceticism in order to seek a path toward heaven (no longer average, but synthetic), where the whole dynamism of matter and the flesh passes over into the genesis of the Spirit.

When, in all inner sincerity, someone on a certain day decides (as *anyone* in quest of sanctity will be obliged to do more and more) to let the upward-moving faith in God and the forward-moving faith in the ultrahuman react freely upon each other in the depths of himself, this someone will sometimes be seized with fright (without being able to call a halt) before the novelty, the boldness and, at the same time, the parodoxical possibility of the attitudes one finds oneself

[19] "Le phénomène humain," 1930.

intellectually and sentimentally forced to take if one wishes to remain faithful to one's fundamental orientations: namely, to attain heaven through the fulfillment of the earth.

Christify matter.

The whole of my inner life was a great and splendid adventure — in the course of which I still often continue to be afraid — but which it was impossible for me not to risk: so powerful was the force with which the layers of the universal and the personal drew near to each other and gradually closed themselves above my head in a single vault.[20]

Let us translate it into biblical language: "I do not ask you to abandon the world but to preserve it from evil." "Every tree that does not bear good fruit is cut down." "Working together with him we entreat you not to receive the grace of God in vain."

God said to Abraham: "Leave your country, your kinfolk, and your father's house for the land which I will show you: I will make a great nation of you" (Gen. 12:1).

Perhaps, within a few centuries, when the uncertainties of Teilhard's vocabulary and scholastic dispute will have fallen into a secondary place — Teilhard will appear, like St. Teresa of Ávila and St. John of the Cross in our day — as a Christian offered as a model to the people. And the discovery of sanctity will resume its mortifying march forward.

[20] "Le cœur de la matière," 1950.

CHAPTER II

Quaestiones Disputatae

"Metaphysics," as we have said, occupies a very small place in Teilhard's work. The first writings, dating from the First World War, are certainly metaphysical and mystical "speculations." But very soon Teilhard found his proper sphere and order of reflection — "physics."

Nevertheless, up to the very end of his life, Teilhard remained faithful to a certain number of metaphysical theses — perceptible in his conversations, correspondence and in some paragraphs of his writings — which it is important to examine briefly. Metaphysics constitutes only an appendix to Teilhard's work. In a text dated 1948 [1] Teilhard gives us the essence of his metaphysics — in four pages!

Teilhard's scientific and mystical work is great enough so that one can freely criticize this complementary part, this annex to his œuvre, that contains his metaphysical ideas. Metaphysics is a technical science which requires of anyone approaching it that he make it his profession. All the evidence indicates that metaphysics was not Teilhard's profession nor, for that matter, was theology, in the technical sense of the word. And Teilhard himself was the very first to admit this.

1. Creation

Let us summarize Teilhard's position on this point. In the very act by which He poses Himself, God opposes Himself trinitarily to Himself. God Himself "exists only in uniting Himself." [2] But by the very fact that He unifies with Himself in order

[1] "Comment je vois," 1948.
[2] *Ibid.*

89

to exist, the First Being causes *ipso facto* another kind of opposition to spring up, no longer at the heart but at His antipode. This is the pure Many or "creatable nothingness" which is nothing, but which, however, through the passive virtuality of arrangement (i.e., of union) is a possibility, an imploration to be.[3] "The fundamental vision is that of plurality and the Multitude."[4]

In 1917 Teilhard wrote: "The working energy of the world, in the beginnings, must be pictured as at grips with an infinite pulverization, a thing which by its very nature (and therefore by tendency) is infinitely disunited, a kind of pure Many. The problem and the secret of creation consisted in reducing and reversing this power of disunion in such a manner so as to obtain monads of a more and more synthetic kind. The more a union has been intimately realized between the most varied elements (in addition to the Multitude to be conquered) the more perfect and conscious being becomes. *Plus esse—plus et a pluribus, uniri.*"[5]

This theorem, which Teilhard maintained and reasserted up to the end, proceeds quite naturally from the law of recurrence discovered in the history of cosmogenesis and biogenesis. Extrapolation consists in the fact that Teilhard posits the existence of a Many infinitely united *previous to our experience* of the process of unification.

In the beginning, therefore, at the two poles of being were God and the Multitude. God, however, was quite alone because the Multitude, sovereignly united, did not exist. From all eternity God saw the scattered shadow of His unity at His feet. This shadow, although itself being an absolute aptitude to give forth something, was not at all another God, because it itself was not. Nor had it ever been nor could it ever have been because its essence was to be infinitely divided in itself; it banded itself about Nothingness. Infinitely vast and infinitely rarified, the Many, annihilated by virtue of its very essence, slumbered at the antipode of single and concentrated Being. . . . It was

[3] "Comment je vois."
[4] "L'union créatrice," 1917.
[5] "La lutte contre la multitude," 1917.

then that unity overflowing with life entered, through creation, into a struggle against the nonexistent Many which was arrayed against it as a contrast and a challenge. To create, according to our *probabilities*, is to condense, concentrate, organize, unify.

Thus Teilhard revives the Aristotelian concept of *matter*, defined as *potential being*. It is the same in Teilhard's later writings, for example in his "Comment je vois" written in 1948: "The pure, antipodal Many is nothing but pure potentiality." [6] The idea of a "struggle" between the One and the Many recalls those Babylonian cosmogonies where we see the demiurge engage in a struggle with chaos. We are deep in metaphysical mythology here. Teilhard, moreover, is in good company since he has taken his place alongside Anaxagoras and Aristotle.

However much the establishment of a law of recurrence, which shows how creation makes itself, as it were by uniting, is legitimate and clarifying, a backward extrapolation, which posits a pure Many as a *potentiality of being* awaiting a creative formation, smacks of those illusions of pure reason the vanity of which has been established by the Kantian critique. Experimentally we know, as Teilhard recognizes and as did Aristotle and St. Thomas before him, only concrete material beings en-

---

[6] "Comment je vois," no. 29. Analogous texts are found in his first writings: "Whereas, true growth takes place in the direction of unity, the least being increases with crumbling. At the moment of their vanishing, things appear to us in a state of division, that is to say, supreme multiplicity. Then they disappear on the side of pure number. They are engulfed in the Many. Being/nothing merges with the completely realized. Pure nothingness is a completely empty concept, a pseudo-idea. *True nothingness, physical nothingness*, that which is on the threshold of being, that upon which all possible worlds converge through their base, is the pure Many, the Multitude" ("La lutte contre la multitude," 1917).

"Since the most material being is the being nearest to the 'pure unifiable' *concrete matter* will appear under the form of the *highly dispersed*. Thus by virtue of its materiality the primitive state of the Cosmos is that of an immense Many, an extreme *Diffused* and *Distended*. Or, more exactly, there is no *precise* beginning to concrete matter: It emerges from an abyss of growing disunity; in some fashion it condenses, starting from an exterior and dark sphere of infinite plurality whose limitless and formless immensity represents the lower pole of being. As soon as we come to recognize some consistency in it, we find that it is formed of an aggregate of monads each of which has already undergone, and bears within itself, an indefinite sum of unions" ("Les noms de la matière," 1919).

dowed with form; there exists no "pure matter" in our experience. This is a concept which proceeds from a retrospective advance of the analysis of the concrete.

Teilhard was very much aware of the difficulties raised by his vision of the pure Many which awaits the formative creativity of God:

I do not conceal from myself that this conception of a sort of *positive nothingness*, as the ground of creation, gives rise to *serious objections*. However banded together about nonbeing as one may posit the Thing, disunited by nature, which is required for the action of creative union, it signifies that the Creator has found outside Himself a fulcrum, or at least a reaction. Thereby it implies that the Creation was not absolutely gratuitous, but represents a motivated work of almost absolute self-interest. All this "redolet Manichaeismum."

It is true. But is it possible, sincerely, to avoid these reefs (or rather these paradoxes) without falling into purely *verbal* explanations? [7]

In a metaphysics of an Alexandrian type, the Many is born of a fall and dispersion of the One, of a procession starting from the One. In a vision of the world in evolution, the One appears as something constituting itself progressively through a synthesis of the Many. This evolutive perspective can be integrated by neo-Platonic metaphysics. It suffices to posit that the actual phase of evolution, historically ascertained, is but the *reparation* of a former, nonhistorical (since history is its effect) phase of *involution*. Actual evolution would be only the return to a former state lost through a mythical fall. We shall see, in connection with original sin, that Teilhard examined this hypothesis (which is, moreover, purely gratuitous and mythological). Alexandrian metaphysics places the Many at the terminus of the procession. Teilhard, extrapolating *a parte ante*, places it at the beginning of the process of evolution. Matter is the host of extremely dispersed elements — and within limits, extension itself? — which God unifies and assembles.

The criticism which Teilhard addresses to the "classic" (i.e.,

[7] "L'union créatrice," 1917.

the scholastic), commonly presented, idea of creation is that it emphasizes to excess the gratuitousness, and arbitrariness of creation. The sufficiency of God entails the radical contingency of the world. And this radical "uselessness" of the world, Teilhard asserts, reveals itself as virulent and dangerous from the moment in which man recognizes that he is called upon to participate in the work of creation. Human action finds itself undermined from the start by this idea that the world, ontologically, is superfluous.[8] "In a metaphysics of union, on the contrary, if the self-sufficiency and self-determination of the Absolute Being remain intact (since I insist that the pure, antipodal Many is only pure potentiality and passivity) in return the creative act takes on a perfectly definite significance and structure. In some way it is the fruit of a reflection of God, no longer in Him, but outside Him, i.e., Pleromization* (to use a word St. Paul might have coined, which is the realization of the participated being through arrangement and totalization) appears as a sort of reply or symmetry to 'Trinitization.' It fills a void, in some fashion. It finds its place."[9] "In the world viewed as the object of 'creation,' classical metaphysics accustoms us to see a sort of extrinsic production, issuing from the supreme *efficiency* of God through an overflow of benevolence. *Invincibly* — and *precisely* in order to be able to act and to love fully at one and the same time — I am now led to see therein (in conformity with the spirit of St. Paul) a mysterious product of completion and fulfillment for the Absolute Being Himself. No longer is it the participated being, situated *ad extra, and characterized by divergence, but the participated Being of pleromization and of convergence.* This is no longer the effect of causality, but of creative union!"[10]

In order to avoid the Charybdis of a universe created in a

---

[8] "Contingence de l'univers et goût humain de survivre," 1953.

[9] "Comment je vois."

[10] "Le cœur de la matière." The appeal to the thought of St. Paul appears forced to us.

---

* *(From pleroma [Gr.]: fullness; in theology, the fullness of divine excellence. — Tr.)*

purely contingent and arbitrary way, Teilhard falls into the Scylla of a well-known mythology. According to it God fulfills Himself in creating the world. God engages in a struggle with the Many (the ancient chaos) in order to find Himself again, richer and pacified, at the terminus of this work. This is an old gnostic idea which is found in Boehme, Hegel and Schelling.

Once again Teilhard falls victim to the inevitable antinomies of pure reason. His criticism of what he rejects is valid, but the solution which he proposes does not seem to be better than the thesis he rejects.

2. The Problem of Evil

Evil, according to Teilhard proceeds from the Many, it constitutes an integral part of the process of an evolutive creation at the base of the Many, and this *by construction*. Thus we cannot consider evil as an accident, nor imagine a creation without evil.

Not at all because of impotence . . . but by virtue of the *very structure of nothingness* over which He leans, God, in order to create, can proceed only *in one way*: namely by arranging and gradually unifying, under His attractive influence, an immense multitude of numbers which are at first infinitely numerous, extremely simple and barely conscious, then gradually more rarified and more complex, and finally endowed with reflection. Now what is the inevitable counterpart of any success obtained from a process of this kind, if not that of having to pay for a certain proportion of waste? Among these we might number: physical disharmonies or putrefactions in the domain of the preliving, suffering in the domain of the living, and sin in domain of freedom. There is no order in the process of formation which at all stages does not imply disorder. And there is nothing in this ontological condition (or more exactly ontogenic) of the participated being which detracts from the dignity or limits the omnipotence of the Creator. Finally there is nothing at all here that "smacks" of anything like Manichaeanism. In itself the pure unorganized Many is not evil. But because it is multiple, that is to say subject essentially to the play of chance in its arrangements, it cannot progress absolutely toward unity without engendering evil here or there — through *statistical necessity*. "Necessarium est ut adveniant scandalas." If, as I believe must inevitably be admitted, there is with

God's point of view. We do not have the right to say that God "could" or "could not" create *the world without evil.* We can only note the following fact : the world is so constructed that evil and death form an integral part of it. We are back again to the antinomies.

Let us also note in passing that in Revelation we do not find any trace of an attempt to "explain" evil. The Book of Job seems to have been written expressly to tell us that it is impossible either to explain or justify evil. Job is a refutation of all theodicy of the Leibnizian variety. Certain texts of the New Testament are equally explicit in this respect : If this or that person is blind or paralytic it is not because he or his fathers have sinned.

On this point still Teilhard justly rejects an idea which, whatever one may think, is not of Christian origin. "According to 'classical' views suffering is a 'punishment' above all, its efficaciousness is that of a sacrifice in that being born of sin sacrifice makes atonement for it." [13] On the contrary, according to the idea dear to Teilhard, "suffering is above all the consequence and the price of the *travail of development*." [14]

This is the suffering of a world which gives birth laboriously and which, in its entirety, as St. Paul wrote, groans and travails in pain until humanity arrives at the perfect stature of Christ.

Given these conditions Redemption does not appear like the *reparation* of an *accident* that befell the creative plan of God. The Incarnation and Redemption constitute an integral part of the creative design of God : The world is created in the Word and the Word becomes flesh in order to bring creation to its terminus. By becoming flesh the Word assumes "the sin of the world," and the Cross makes manifest this inevitable law: Creation takes place through failure and sorrow. Christ, through the Cross, assumes the law of *all* creation. Creation, Incarnation and Redemption are indivisible in fact. Teilhard follows Duns Scotus here. To the juridical conception of Redemption, Teilhard prefers a conception of Redemption received from the

[13] "La vie cosmique," 1916.
[14] *Ibid.*

Greek fathers and the great Franciscan tradition. Far from forgetting the mystery of the Cross, as certain people have charged, Teilhard's originality is that he sees the mystery of the Cross operating everywhere in creation. This was his constant position from his first to his last writings. "While marking a higher stage in the gratuitousness of the divine operation, are not creation, the Incarnation and Redemption each so many acts indissolubly linked in the apparition of participated being?" [15] "And it is in this way that step by step a series of notions which for a long time were regarded as independent, come to link themselves together organically under our very eyes. . . . There is no creation without an incarnating immersion, no Incarnation without a redemptive compensation. In a metaphysics of union the three fundamental 'mysteries' of Christianity are but three aspects of the mystery of mysteries, that of 'Pleromization.' And, at the same time, it discloses a renewed Christology, no longer only the historical or juridical axis, but the structural axis, of all theology." [16]

[15] "L'âme du monde," 1918.
[16] "Comment je vois," 1948.

CHAPTER 12

Conclusions and Reflections

The misinterpretations of Teilhard's work are numerous. There is nothing surprising about this if one reflects on the novelty of his thought and on the fact that the greater part of it has remained unpublished to this day.

As has already been noted by Msgr. Bruno de Solages,[1] these misinterpretations and misunderstandings, in the majority of cases, arise from the fact that the reader of Teilhard's texts does not place himself on the same plane of observation from which Teilhard wrote. Let us say more precisely that the reader and, in particular, the theological reader especially does not sufficiently distinguish between what one might call the diverse "literary genres" among Teilhard's multiple writings: the one purely technical and paleontological, the other basically mystical and theological. Often the reader does sufficiently take into account the *plane* on which this or that text, which they have the good fortune to read, is situated.

On the scientific side the criticism most frequently formulated upon coming across his writings which present a scientific synthesis ("a *Weltanschauung*") is that they go beyond the limits permitted by the strict rigor of scientific method. On this question we refer the reader to the book we have already mentioned, François Meyer's work, in which this particular epistemological problem is analyzed: It is permissible for a scientist to attempt a general phenomenology of evolution? Rejection of Teilhard's theses in this respect, it seems to us, often stems from the fact that the specialist, working at the level of the micro-phenomenon, is unable to grasp the validity of work performed

[1] Cf. *supra*, pp. 16–17.

on the plane of the macrophenomenon. Quite probably one refuses to grant a scientific character to Teilhard's effort because it occurs at the level of a phenomenological analysis which investigates the direction of the total spatio-temporal phenomenon. Here, without a doubt, for some scientists, certain of their philosophical presuppositions are an obstacle to an understanding of his work. These more or less explicit philosophical presuppositions might be expressed as follows: The real, because real, cannot have any *direction* at all; the investigation of the direction of evolution is no longer, and can never be, science —it is metaphysics. But, on the other hand, we may note that all modern psychology testifies to the fact that one *can* make an attempt to elucidate the direction of a phenomenon while at the same time remaining strictly within the limits of scientific method. To one who is conversant with Teilhard's work—and insofar as one is at home with this *Weltanschauung* — the elucidation of the direction of the cosmic and biological phenomenon attempted by Teilhard is scientific, that is to say valid. In the beginning the ideas of Galileo and Einstein must have also seemed too fantastic to be scientific. But, as Teilhard has noted, modern physics has taught us that only the fantastic has a chance of being true. The future will tell whether Teilhard's synthesis is truly scientific. The mind becomes used to a new vision of the world as the ear to a musical esthetic and the eye to a type of painting that are original. Scientific sanction, there, as elsewhere, is retrospective.

From the theological side the criticisms directed against Teilhard have revolved around questions of the "supernatural" and "original sin."

Teilhard, most frequently, applied himself to a description of "appearances" which is the scientific point of view. On certain points he recognizes that he has extrapolated, as it is legitimate to do; as an example, we cite the elucidation of the center of Omega convergence. But he remained on the empirical level of phenomenology. He applied himself to speaking the language of the modern world, and more particularly the language of scientific research. And he could not do otherwise since he most often addressed himself to scientists. The necessity of this approach is evident even from a missionary point of view. A missionary of the Church in China addresses himself to the natives in Chinese. To the extent — and this was considerable — in which Teilhard's concern was constantly a missionary one, it would be absurd to criticize Teilhard for not taking into account, in his writings addressed to unbelievers, metaphysical or theological certitudes which the latter would specifically not admit.

In his scientific synthesis Teilhard applied himself to sorting out a law of recurrence which would define the stages of the history of the world and of life up to and including man : Cosmogenesis, biogenesis, anthropogenesis. In short "a history of creation."

Teilhard applied himself with great care to marking out and underlining the critical *thresholds* where the real passes from one state to another, to a higher order, and one irreducibly new. Thus if a metaphysician or theologian criticizes Teilhard for not dealing, in connection with each critical threshold, with the special creative intervention which operates — be it at the apparition of life, of consciousness, or of the soul supernaturally adapted to theological life — it is they who are confusing planes and "formal objects." In a phenomenological presentation, Teilhard *did not have to deal* with the metaphysical causality which operates within second and experimental causes. But if he did, that is, if Teilhard in this connection spoke of "creation," of "spirit" (in a specifically Christian sense) then one would be justified in criticizing Teilhard — and the scientists would not fail to do so — for confusing orders of knowledge which are irreducibly distinct.

And if Teilhard is criticized for not, as a metaphysician would desire, sufficiently bringing into relief the element of human freedom in the process of socialization and anthropogenesis which he describes, it is because of similar confusion of the orders of reflection. When a sociologist establishes a statistical

law dealing with suicide or marriage he is under no obligation
to deal with the element of human freedom which comes to play
in every suicide, and in every decision. He does not thereby deny
human freedom. But the human freedom which he analyzes, on
the plane on which he analyzes it, is a statistical phenomenon
which does not require the intervention of the metaphysical
question concerning freedom. The psychologist will approach
the phenomenon of suicide or marriage on another plane, at
another level, and he will incline toward the individual decisions
which preceded the accomplishment of the particular act (mi-
crophenomenon). The metaphysician finally will apply himself
to ascertain the role played by human freedom within the framework of biological, psychological, sociological and other deter-
minants. These different approaches are neither contradictory
nor incompatible with one another: they are complementary.
When the statistician informs us that a certain number of automobile accidents will take place during a certain weekend, he is
not obliging anybody to get himself killed in an automobile.

Teilhard studies the real at the level of the macrophenomenon, at the statistical level. It is up to the philosopher to utilize
the data uncovered by Teilhard's research in order to integrate
them within a metaphysical synthesis. Teilhard expressly
limited himself to an investigation at a *physical* level.

As regards the "supernatural" we have tried to show that
Teilhard describes, at the level of appearances and with the
means at the disposal of modern science, the *natural conditions*
— cosmic, biological, anthropological — which prepare a *supernatural* fulfillment. These conditions, it must be said, *do not
constitute* the supernatural fulfillment which they prepare. The
physical, sociological, political, and mental convergence of humanity on itself does not provide, in itself, an atom of charity.
This is of another and supernatural order. But the unification of
humanity prepares, and permits, this unity of the Mystical Body
which is realized in a supernatural way by the Holy Ghost and
the indwelling of the Word in the Church, its spouse.

Thus one cannot reproach Teilhard for having confused

planes (natural and supernatural), not only because of the place he expressly reserves for the supernatural but, even more, because he shows the cosmic, biological and human preparations for its apparition. All creation tends toward its supernatural end which it desires: *desiderium naturale sed inefficax videndi Deum*. Teilhard's entire work might be defined as an effort to describe, positively, this desire of creation which tends toward its Creator. From a metaphysical point of view evolution and time are like the expression of a still unsatisfied desire which tends toward its terminus. It is the messianic waiting of all creation, not only of Israel, but of all the universe, of the entire cosmogenesis.

Here too, if the theologian criticizes Teilhard for not having dealt with this supernatural order, he would be demanding that Teilhard confuse the planes of research and the orders of knowledge. Teilhard, in his scientific work, did not have to deal with the supernatural gift made to the creature. This is the concern of the theologian. And an evolutive vision of creation would be of great benefit to the theologian for the theological understanding of the relations between the creation of God and the Gift of God to His creation.

If the theologian deplores that the Omega Point, in Teilhard's synthesis, is not more explicitly named, this too results from a misunderstanding over method. In a phenomenological analysis the Omega Point can only be an algebraic sign which expresses the *requirement* — the *desire* — of all creation. Only the Gift, the *fact* of the Incarnation permits us to name the One for whom all creation waits, and the Gift surpasses everything that creation could desire.

As regards original sin, two things must be distinguished: in his scientific writings (as has been remarked previously) Teilhard, as is obvious, was under no obligation to deal with original sin. In the few unpublished notes which he devoted to original sin, Teilhard poses questions and pronounces opinions that it is permissible for theologians to criticize. Indeed nothing could be more legitimate! But what is absurd is to reproach Teilhard for not showing the place and the action of original sin in his scientific synthesis! This again is the task of the theologian and not of the scientist. In the notes which he wrote on the subject of original sin, Teilhard propounds the question: How does the representation of original sin [as taught to Teilhard] find a place in what we call human history? I say, be it noted, the representation taught to Teilhard, and not the dogma of original sin. Here is a sociological fact which has had serious consequences for Teilhard: Teilhard was provided with a particular theological teaching which led him to pose insoluble problems. This is not the place to examine the metaphysics and theology which in fact were taught to young Teilhard. (The task, by the way, would not be profitless, as we know from the case of Descartes.)

We conclude by distinguishing the "literary genres" among Teilhard's writings. Nothing is more in order than for a theologian to criticize theological writings in the name of theology. But it is exorbitant to demand of Teilhard that, in his scientific writings, he resolve all the theological problems occasioned by modern science!

As regards monogenism, finally, let us recall — if this be still necessary — that science as such does not deal with individual particulars. Modern physics does not concern itself with this or that particular electron or corpuscle: they are indiscernible. Modern physics, in essence, is *statistical*. Biology, likewise, does not concern itself with individuals but with *species* and phyletic populations. Thus the question of monogenism (are there one or several individuals at the origin of the human species?) as such is not a biological question. Science nowadays leans strongly toward monophyletism (the original unity of the human species). But it can have nothing to say about monogenism, for the question does not fall within its competence. In any case, it remains to be determined, first of all, what one understands, metaphysically speaking, by the concept of *man*. Theologically speaking, must not man be defined as a creature called upon to participate in the life of God? In this case human *nature* would be defined principally by its *supernatural vocation*. In a herd of anthropoids a scientist would find it impossible to determine which one among them was called to this supernatural destiny which defines man in Christian terms.

There remain on the balance sheet against Teilhard certain uncertainties of vocabulary in his writings which are strictly metaphysical and theological. But these texts are few. We ourselves have not refrained from firmly criticizing certain of Father Teilhard's metaphysical propositions.

But let us recall here that metaphysics occupies only a secondary place in Teilhard's work: the few metaphysical theses that Teilhard maintains are deduced from his scientific vision of the world by an inference which to us appeared illegitimate. It is not metaphysics, however, but experimental science and mystical experience which occupy first place in Teilhard's thought.

Thus we can reply, in a few words, to the questions posed at the beginning of this study. What is the initial "contact," the live and germinal "intuition" which explains Teilhard's work?

1) The scientific discovery of the fact of evolution: The real is a phenomenon in development, in a process of oriented evolution, in genesis. Metaphysically speaking, this signifies that creation, which is still unfinished, continues under our very eyes.

2) The experience of a lack of balance between the most legitimate demands of adoration, present at the heart of this world in gestation, and certain of the morbid forms of spirituality erroneously presented as Christian. Christianity cannot fire the modern world unless it understands the divine nature of the work which is in progress in all creation, and of which human work constitutes the last stage; and it must participate as a pioneer in the human research which tends not only toward well-being but first and foremost toward *more-being*, that is to say toward bringing about the accomplishment of the plenitude of the stature of man.

3) Creation cannot fulfill itself unless man recognizes before him Christ, Alpha and Omega, whose co-inheritor he is called upon to become. The whole of creation manifests the waiting

and desire for the One who is coming. The world cannot fulfill itself except in adoration. Love is not only a sentiment, but the energy which alone can permit creation to arrive at its terminus.

If the formulations of Teilhard's theological thought are sometimes defective, the thought itself, on the contrary, rediscovers the great current of biblical, apostolic, and patristic tradition. (Let us in particular note the kinship between Teilhard's theological thought and that of St. Irenaeus and St. Gregory of Nyssa.)

A work cannot be judged on fragments, nor on partial texts separated from the whole. It is possible, without doubt, to find in the work of St. Augustine, for example, certain texts and even certain entire treatises which nowadays appear "heretical." But a work can be only understood when taken in its organic totality, like a person, that is to say in the living thought which informs and animates it, in the spirit that is at its beginning and end. The offense of certain Augustinians has been to extract according to their tastes partial texts from the total work of St. Augustine. But St. Augustine is thereby no less a doctor of the Church.

The spirit which animates Teilhard's work is the love of the living Christ for whom all creation sighs, and in whom it will find its fulfillment and consistency; this is the adoration which science discovers each day more and more throughout all creation. "Thou shalt love the Lord thy God with thy whole heart, with thy whole soul, and with thy whole mind." Teilhard knew how to make his science contribute to his love and adoration.

By virtue of this, Teilhard's work merits more than the unfair quarrels conducted by his disciples or adversaries, who confine themselves to its partial aspects. Let us hope that the lesson of the past may serve us and that, as St. Paul demands, we may know how to "prove all things" and "hold fast that which is good." [2]

[2] 1 Thess. 5:21.

A Glossary

Prepared by Rev. Robert Francoeur

ANTHROPOGENESIS. The course by which evolution gives birth to individual man, his family, and to tribal, national and international bonds on a purely physical or psychological level. *See* Christogenesis.

AUTOEVOLUTION. The human stage of evolution in which after a long history of "imposed" or unconscious evolving the progress of evolution becomes "conscious of itself" through the appearance of reflective human beings who can now control their own advance along the path to the Omega Point.

BIOGENESIS. The "birth" evolution underwent in giving rise to life in all its various shapes and forms. *See* Christogenesis.

BIOSPHERE. The realm of life, the layer of living things which forms a "covering" over the world.

CEPHALIZATION. The process by which evolution gradually increases the amount of nervous tissue in organisms the further along in time that they appear, and in the same stroke centralizes this tissue in the brain case.

CHRISTOGENESIS. The fourth in a series of "_____geneses"; a term coined by Teilhard to describe the fourth stage of the evolutionary universe: cosmogenesis, the birth of the universe; biogenesis, the birth of life; anthropogenesis, the birth of individual human beings; and Christogenesis, the birth of ultrasynthesized mankind, the Mystical Body of Christ: the birth of the "Whole Christ."

COMPLEXITY. The result of a cosmic drift or flow of matter, in opposition to the flow of entropy; "an organized heterogeneity"; a group of different elements arranged and organized in a definite number without aggregation, as in a sand pile, or repetition, as in a crystal. Examples of various complexities are the atom, molecule, cell, protozoon, animal, plant, and human.

107

COMPLEXITY/CONSCIOUSNESS. One of the two basic laws of evolution, the other being the Law of Entropy. It is the curve that evolution followed from the sub-atomic stage, where complexity and consciousness were at a minimum, to man, where they are at their greatest.

CONCRESCENCE. An embryological term which Teilhard uses to indicate the gradual "growing together" of separate things as evolution progresses. This involves interaction and relationships that are important in the advance of evolution.

CONE OF TIME. The triangle formed by life as it rises from the most dispersed and unconscious elements of the subatomic to the most conscious and centralized elements of the "Cosmic Body of Christ." "Cone of Time" is a figure of speech to which Teilhard often adds the adjective "truncated," that is, an evolution which stops with modern man and ignores spiritual destiny, an evolution without a final point of convergence, without an apex.

CONSCIOUSNESS. For Teilhard this word had many meanings. Throughout his writings he maintained that consciousness is co-extensive with all material things. In its own way, the cell is "conscious of its environment." It reacts to its surroundings. Richet called it "cellular consciousness." In the insect world, instincts are "consciousness imprisoned in a chitinous shell." The animal "only knows" while man "knows that he knows." Man has consciousness in the normal sense of the word, reflective thought capable of moral decisions. But for Teilhard even the inorganic possesses consciousness though it is extremely dispersed and nonfunctional.

CORPUSCULIZATION. A parallel term for "interiorized" and "arranged," corpusculization is the result of one of the fundamental cosmic currents, namely, "complexity/consciousness." Basically it is the direction or process evolution takes in increasing the complexity and consciousness of organisms as they appear at the head of the evolutionary stream.

COSMIC BODY. The full meaning of the Mystical Body of Christ in which all creatures, rational, irrational and inanimate will be consummated, where "God will be All in All."

COSMIC DRIFT. The direction and flow that matter or the evolutionary stream follows with the passage of time. *See* Privileged Axis.

COSMOGENESIS. The birth or evolution of the mineral and inorganic world. *See* Christogenesis.

DIFFERENTIATED UNION. The final synthesis of all human beings in the Cosmic Body of Christ. It is a union which includes all creatures though the emphasis is on humans. Differentiated because this is not a union based on an impersonalized materialistic love that destroys individuality and personality. The differentiated union perfects the elements synthesized, preserves their individuality and personality while lifting them to a new and higher level of existence.

ENTROPY. The second principle of thermodynamics whereby there is a constant degradation of utilizable energy available in the universe. Matter is thus on an irreversible downgrade toward motionlessness and absolute cold. Entropy is the cosmic force which constantly fights against the rise of complexity/consciousness. The curve formed by these two opposing forces is the "curve of corpusculization."

HOMINIZATION. For Teilhard the word meant all the processes and events which followed the appearance of man in our world and led to the socialization, intermingling and interrelating of all mankind on the natural level.

HUMAN ENERGETICS. *See* Problem of Action.

HUMAN MONADS. Biologists use the term "monad" to refer to any simple, single-cell organism. Teilhard transfers this meaning to the individual human being, paralleling the relation of the single cell to the organism with that of the single human to the superorganism of the Mystical Body of Christ.

INTERIORIZATION. "The process of turning in on oneself." For Teilhard this term means the process of evolution by which it became conscious of itself, by which the forces of evolution were slowly transferred from the exterior to the interior. Evolutionary emphasis changed from the physical to the psychic and spiritual. In man this would also imply the gradual centralization and concentration of the brain in the skull case.

MONAD. *See* Human Monad.

NOOSPHERE. The realm of the mind or reflective thought, the layer of thinking creatures — humans — who gradually spread over the surface of the world.

OMEGA POINT. For Teilhard the "scientific Omega Point" represents the final focal point of convergence of the material and spiritual world. It is a scientific extrapolation from the phenomena of our world and coincides perfectly with the Incarnate Christ in whom "all will find their consistence."

PANTOCRATOR. A biblical term referring to Christ as the Creator of all things. Teilhard's explanation of evolution with Christ, the Omega Point, at the apex of the temporal-spatial phenomenon, the Cone of Time, strengthens and increases the realism of the "Creator of all things."

PHENOMENOLOGY. Husserl and other modern philosophers have used this term in an entirely different sense than that given the term by Teilhard. To him it meant a science which drew its knowledge and facts, not from the minute studies of specialists, but from the over-all picture of concrete appearances of the world. It is the ancient Greek "Physics," but it certainly is not a "philosophy."

PLENITUDE. A biblical term used very often to refer to the end of the World, the final stage of the material universe when creation will reach its fullness (pleroma) in God, the time when "God will be All in All."

POLARIZATION. This word has several meanings: a trend of thought, a general outlook, or, more often, the direction in which a particular stream of evolution flows, i.e., the "privileged axis."

PRIVILEGED AXIS. This term refers to the zig-zag line evolution has taken in its course to the human stage. It refers to the main line of evolution where the law of complexity/consciousness is most important. The side branches, the dead ends, like the dinosaurs, are not in the privileged axis. They are off-shoots which have left the main stream only to be lost.

PROBLEM OF ACTION. The problem which arises in our modern day. Man has lost all hope of the future and ceased, in many cases, from sharing in conscious evolution. Since evolution can now only mean man's advance toward the ultrahuman and since this advance can only be accomplished with man's cooperation, the problem is to overcome this despair and stir men to action.

SUPEREGO. The outcome of the ultrapersonalized individual, the individual person united to Christ in the Cosmic Body. *See* Differentiated Union.

ULTRAPHYSICS OF THE UNION. An extrapolation from the "physics of synthesis" by which electrons, protrons and neutrons are united in an atom, atoms are united in molecules, etc. The ultraphysics is concerned with the synthesis of human individuals into a new and higher body, the Mystical Body.

UNION. The arrangement of elements or monads in a synthesis which gives the participants a higher and new level of consciousness as well as a higher degree of complexity.

UNROLLED. A general term referring to the whole history of evolution, both spiritual and physical, in the direction of greater concentration, complexity and consciousness.

Bibliography

Prepared by Rev. Robert Francoeur

---

1. By Teilhard *

1909. "Les miracles de Lourdes et les enquêtes canoniques," *Études*, 118 (1909), 161–83.

1911. "L'homme devant les enseignements de l'Église et devant la philosophie spiritualiste," *Dictionnaire apologétique de la foi Catholique*, II (1911), 501–14.

1913. "La préhistoire et ses progrès," *Études*, 134 (1913), 40–53; *L'apparition de l'homme*, p. 21–38.

1916. "La maîtrise du monde."

"Sur quelques primates des phosphorites du Quercy," *Annales de paléontologie*, 10 (1916), 1–20.

"La vie cosmique."

"Les mammifères de l'eocène inferieur français et leur gisements," *Annales de paléontologie*, 10 (1916), 171–76; 11 (1921), 1–108; *Les mammifères de l'eocène inferieur français et leur gisements*. Paris: Masson, 1922[?].

1917. "L'union créatrice."

"Mon univers."

"La lutte contre la multitude."

"Nostalgie du front"; *La table ronde*, 90 (1955), 64–67.

1918. "L'âme du monde."

1919. "Les noms de la matière."

1920. "Note sur le progrès."

1920[?] "Note sur les modes de l'action divine dans l'univers."

* For a more systematic bibliography, see that prepared by C. Cuénot in his work cited below.

112

1921.　"Les hommes fossiles, à propos d'un livre récent," *Études,* 166 (1921), 570–77; *L'apparition de l'homme,* pp. 39–55.

"Comment se pose aujourd'hui la question du transformisme," *Études,* 167 (1921), 524–44; *La vision du passé,* pp. 15–40.

"La face de la terre," *Études,* 169 (1921), 585–602; *La vision du passé,* pp. 41–69.

1923.　"La messe en esprit"; *La table ronde,* 90 (1955), 29–30. / "La messe sur la monde" (Ordos).

"L'hominisation, introduction a une étude scientifique du phénomène humain" (May 6); *La vision du passé,* pp. 77–111.

"La paléontologie et l'apparition de l'homme," *Revue de philosophie,* 30 (1923), 53–80; *L'apparition de l'homme,* pp. 51–81.

"Sur la loi d'irréversibilité en évolution," *L'anthropologie,* 33 (1923); *La vision du passé,* pp. 73–74.

1923—.　*Lettres de voyage, 1923–1939.* Paris: Grasset, 1956.

1924.　"On the Discovery of a Paleolithic Industry in Northern China," *Bulletin of the Geological Survey of China,* 3 (1924), 45–50.

1925.　"L'histoire naturelle du monde: réflexions sur le valeur et l'avenir de la systématique," *Scientia,* 37 (1925), 15–24; *La vision du passé,* 145 ff.

With E. LICENT. "Note sur deux instruments agricole du néolithique de Chine," *L'anthropologie,* 35 (1925), 62–74.

With E. LICENT. "Le paléolithique de la Chine," *L'anthropologie,* 35 (1925), 201–34.

"Le paradoxe transformiste, à propos de la dernière critique du transformisme par M. Vialleton," *Revue des questions scientifiques* (4th ser.), 8 (1925); *La vision du passé,* pp. 115–42.

"Observations nouvelles sur les mammifères du tertiaire inférieur de Belgique," *Bulletin de l'Académie de Science de la Belgique,* Classe de science (5th ser.), 11 (1925), 48–50.

114   *Bibliography*

1926.   "Le néolithique de la Chine d'après les découvertes du
         Dr. Anderson," *L'anthropologie*, 36 (1926), 117–24.

         "Sur l'apparence nécessairement discontinue de toute
         série évolutive," *L'anthropologie*, 36 (1926), 320–21;
         La vision du passé, pp. 159–62.

         "Les fondements et le fond de l'idée d'évolution" (Gulf of
         Bengal, Ascension Thursday); *La vision du passé*, pp.
         163–97.

         With E. LICENT and D. BLACK. "On a Presumably Pleis-
         tocene Human Tooth from the Sjaraosso-gol (southeast-
         ern Ordos) deposits," *Bulletin of the Geological Survey
         of China*, 5 (1927), 285–90.

         Étude géographique sur la région du Dalai-Noor. "Mém-
         oirs de la Société géologique de France (NS), t. 3, fasc.
         3." Paris, 1926.

         "Fossil Man in China and Mongolia," translated by C. D.
         MATTHEW, *Natural History*, 26 (1926), 238–45.

1927.   *Les mammifères de l'eocène inférieur de la Belgique.*
         "Mémoirs du Musée Royale d'Histoire Naturelle de Bel-
         gique, no. 36." 1927.

         Le milieu divin; Paris: Seuil, 1957.

1928.   "Note complémentaire sur la fourne de mammifères du
         tertiaire inférieur d'Orsmael," *Bulletin de l'Académie
         Royale Belgique de Science*, 14 (5th ser.), 8–9 (1928),
         471–74.

         "Les mouvements de la vie" (April); *La vision du passé,*
         pp. 201–10.

         With M. BOULE, H. BREUIL and E. LICENT. "Le paléo-
         lithique de la Chine," *Archives de l'Institute de Paléon-
         tologie Humaine*, 4.

1929.   "Le paléolithique en Somalie française et en Abyssinie,"
         L'anthropologie, 40 (1929), 331–34.

         With C. C. YOUNG. "Preliminary Report on the Chou-
         Kou-Tien Fossiliferous Deposit," *Bulletin of the Geo-
         logical Survey of China*, 8 (1929), 173–202.

1930.   "La paléontologie des mammifères en Chine et l'œuvre
         de musée Hoangho-Paiho," *Revue scientifique*, 68
         (1930), 360–62.

"Palaeontology of Mammifers in China," *Irish Ecclesiastical Record*, 36 (1930), 363–69.

"Sinanthropus pekinensis," *Primitive Man*, 3 (1930), 46–48.

"Le sinanthropus de Péking — État actuel de nos connaissances sur le fossile et son gisement," *L'anthropologie*, 41 (1930), 1–11.

"Que faut-il penser du transformisme?" *Revue des questions scientifiques*, 17 (1930), 89–99; *La vision du passé*, pp. 211–23.

"Le phénomène humain," *Revue des questions scientifiques*, 18 (1930), 1–19; *La vision du passé*, pp. 225–43.

"Une importante découverte de paléontologie humain: Le *sinanthropus pekinensis*" (Peking, April), *Revue des questions scientifiques*, 18 (1930), 5–16; *L'apparition de l'homme*, pp. 83–95.

With C. C. YOUNG. *Preliminary Observations on the Pre-Loessic and Post-Pontian Formations in Western Shansi and Northern Shensi*. Peking: Geological Survey of China, 1930.

With W. P. LAMARE, M. DREYFUSS, A. LACROIX and MLLE. É. BASSE, *Études géographiques en Éthiopie, Somalie et Arabie méridionale*. Paris: Société géologique de France, 1930.

1931.　"Some Observations on the Archeological Material Collected by Mr. A. S. Lukashkin near Tsitsihar (Manchuria)," *Bulletin of the Geological Survey of China*, 11 (1931), 183–193.

With C. C. YOUNG. *Fossil Mammals from the Late Cenozoic of Northern China*. Peking: Geological Survey of China, 1931.

"The Spirit of Earth" (Pacific), *Construire la terre*, pp. 57–63.

1932.　With W. C. PEI. "The Lithic Industry of the *Sinanthropus* Deposits in Choukoutien," *Bulletin of the Geological Survey of China*, 11 (1932), 315–58.

With C. C. YOUNG. "On Some Neolithic (and Possibly Paleolithic) Finds in Mongolia, Sinkiang and West

China," *Bulletin of the Geological Survey of China,* 12 (1932), 83–104.

"La place de l'homme dans la nature," *Revue des étudiants de l'Université Nationale de Pékin* (1932); *La vision du passé,* pp. 245–56.

"Les résultats scientifiques de l'expédition Citroën-Centre-Asia," *Terre, Air, Mer.* Paris, 1932. Pp. 379–90.

1933.   "L'incroyance moderne. Cause profonde et remède," *La vie intellectuelle,* 24 (1933), 218–22.

With D. BLACK, C. C. YOUNG and W. C. PEI. *Fossil Man in China — The Choukoutien Cave Deposits with a Synopsis of Our Present Knowledge of the Late Cenozoic in China.* "Memoirs of the Geological Survey of China, Ser. A, no. 11." Peking, 1933.

1934.   "Comment je crois."

With W. C. PEI. "New Discoveries in Choukoutien, 1933–34," *Bulletin of the Geological Survey of China,* 13 (1934), 309–89.

"Les fouilles préhistoriques de Pékin," *Revue des questions scientifiques* (4th ser.), 25 (1934), 181–93; *L'apparition de l'homme,* 97–110.

With R. A. STIRTON. *A Correlation of Some Miocene and Pliocene Mammaliam Assemblages in North America and Asia with a Discussion of the Mio-Pliocene Boundary,* "University of California Publications. Bulletin of the Department of Geological Science, v. 23, no. 8." Berkley, 1934.

1935.   With C. C. YOUNG, W. C. PEI and H. C. CHANG. "On the Cenozoic Formations of Kwangsi and Kwangtung," *Bulletin of the Geological Survey of China,* 14 (1935), 179–205.

"La faune pléistocène et l'ancienneté de l'homme en Amérique du Nord," *L'anthropologie,* 45 (1935), 483–87; *L'apparition de l'homme,* pp. 111–18.

"La découverte du passé" (Red Sea, September 15), *Études,* 231 (1935), 469–78; *La vision du passé,* pp. 257–69.

1936.   With H. DE TERRA. "Observations on the Upper Siwalik Formations and Later Pleistocene Deposits in India,"

Proceedings of the American Philosophical Society, 76 (1936), 791–822.

"Quelques réflexions sur la conversion du monde."

"Esquisse d'un univers personnel."

With C. C. YOUNG. *On the Mammalian Remains from the Archeological Site of Anyang.* Nanking: Geological Survey of China, 1936.

Fossil Mammals from Locality 9 of Choukoutien. Nanking: Geological Survey of China, 1936.

"We Must Save Mankind" (Peking, November 11), *Construire la terre,* pp. 49–56.

1937.   "La crise présent, réflexions d'un naturaliste," *Études,* 233 (1937), 145–65.

"Notes sur la paléontologie humaine en Asie Orientale," *L'anthropologie,* 47 (1937), 22–33.

"The Post-Villafranchian Interval in North China," *Bulletin of the Geological Survey of China,* 17 (1937), 169–75.

"La découverte du sinanthrope," *Études,* 232 (1937), 5–13; *L'apparition de l'homme,* pp. 119–31.

"Le phénomène spirituel."

"L'énergie humaine."

With M. TRASSAERT. *The Proboscidians of South-eastern Shansi.* Nanking: Geological Survey of China, 1937.

"Our Most Ape-like Relative," *Natural History,* 40 (1937), 514–17.

"The Pleistocene of China: Stratigraphy and Correlations," *Early Man.* Philadelphia, 1937. Pp. 211–20.

"Human Energy" (Peking), *Construire la terre,* 64–72.

1938.   "Deuxièmes notes sur la paléontologie humaine en Asie méridionale," *L'anthropologie,* 48 (1938), 449–56.

The Fossils from Locality 12 of Choukoutien. Nanking: Geological Survey of China, 1938.

With M. TRASSAERT. *Cavicornia of Southeastern Shansi.* Nanking: Geological Survey of China, 1938.

"Le Villafranchien d'Asie et la question du Villafranchien," *Compte rendu sommaire du séances, Société Géologique de France,* 17 (1938), pp. 325–27.

1939.   "La mystique de la science," *Études,* 238 (1939), 725–42.

With H. BREUIL and P. WERNERT. "Les industries lithiques de Somalie français," *L'anthropologie,* 49 (1939) 497–522.

"Les unités humaines naturelles: Essai d'une biologie et d'une morale des races," *Études,* 240 (1939), 6–30; *La vision du passé,* pp. 271–301.

1939—.   *Nouvelles lettres de voyage, 1939–1955.* Paris: Grasset, 1957.

1940.   *Le phénomène humain*; Paris: Seuil, 1955; *The Phenomenon of Man.* Translated by Bernard Wall. New York: Harper, 1959.

The Fossils from Locality 18, near Peking. Chungking: Geological Survey of China, 1940.

1941.   *Early Man in China,* "Publications of the Institut de Géo-Biologie, no. 7." Peking, 1941.

Réflexions sur le progrès. Peking, 1941. (Includes "L'avenir de l'homme vu par un paléontologiste" and "Les bases possibles d'un credo humain commun.")

"On the Possibility of a Common Credo" (Peking, March 30), *Construire la terre,* pp. 76–79.

"Thoughts on Progress" (Peking, March 30), *Construire la terre,* pp. 73–74.

"L'avenir de l'homme," *Cité Nouvelle,* June, 1941.

1942.   "L'esprit nouveau."

"La montée de l'autre."

"La place de l'homme dans l'univers, réflexions sur la complexité."

"Note sur la notion de perfection chrétienne."

1943.   "Réflexions sur le bonheur"; *La table ronde,* 90 (1955), 81–86.

"Super-humanité, Super-Christ, Super-charité" (Peking).

"De nouvelles dimensions pour l'avenir."

Fossil Men: Discoveries and Present Problems. Peking:
H. Vetch, 1943; *La question de l'homme fossile: découvertes récentes et problèmes actuels.* Translated by M.
CHOISY. Paris: *Psyché,* 1948; *L'apparition de l'homme,*
pp. 133–74.

1944.   With W. C. PEI. *Le néolithique de la Chine.* "Publications of the Institut de Géo-Biologie, no. 10." Peking,
1944.

"La centrologie."

"Essai d'une dialectique de l'union."

"Introduction à la vie chrétienne."

1945.   "Heredité sociale et éducation," *Études,* 245 (April,
1945).

"Christianisme et évolution."

1946.   "Vie et planètes, que se pense-t-il en ce moment sur la
terre?" *Études,* 249 (1946), 145–69.

"Quelques réflexions sur le retentissement spirituel de la
bombe atomique," *Études,* 250 (1946), 223–30.

"Esquisse d'une dialectique de l'esprit."

"Le Christianisme et la science," *Esprit,* 14 (1946),
253–56.

"Le cone du temps," *Psyché,* (1946), 23–27; 171–99.

"La planetisation humaine," *Cahiers du Monde Nouveau*
(August, 1946).

"L'évolution," *Actes du congrès internationale de Philosophie.* Rome, 1946.

1947.   "Un colloque scientifique sur l'évolution," *Études,* 253
(1957), 257–59.

"Réflexions sur le pêche originel."

"Agitation ou genèse."

"Évolution zoologique et invention," *Paléontologie et
transformisme* (With C. ARAMBOURG et al). Paris: Albin
Michel, 1950. Pp. 233–35; *La vision du passé,* pp.
327–31.

"Une interprétation plausible de l'histoire humain: la
formation de la Noosphère," *Revue des questions scientifiques,* 8 (1947), 7–37.

"Le rebondissement humain de l'évolution et ses conséquences" (St Germain-en-Laye, September 23), *Revue des questions scientifiques*, 9 (1948), 166–85.

"Sur une mandibule de meganthropus," *Compte rendu des séances, Société Géologique de France* (1947), 309–10.

"Le pithecanthrope," *Psyché* (March, 1947), 254–60.

"L'homme du pleistocène," *Psyché* (April, 1947), 423–33.

"La question de l'homme fossile," *Psyché* (February, 1947), 126–34.

"Foi et la paix," *Cahiers du Monde Nouveau* (January, 1947).

1948.   "Socialisation humaine," *L'anthropologie*, 52 (1948), 10.

"Position de l'homme et signification de la socialisation humaine dans la nature," *L'anthropologie,* 52 (1948), 209–19.

"Résumé de la pensée du Père."

"Comment je vois."

"Les directions et les conditions de l'avenir," *Psyché* (October, 1948), 981–91.

"Les conditions de l'unification humaine," *Psyché* (December, 1948), 8; "Psychological Conditions for Human Unification," *Cross Currents*, 3 (1952), 1–5.

1949.   "Le cœur du problème" (Les Moulins, September 8).

"L'humanité se muet-elle biologiquement sur elle-même? (St Germain-en-Laye, May 4), *Revue des questions scientifiques*, 10 (1949), 498–516.

Le groupe zoologique humain: structure et directions évolutives; Paris: Michel, 1956.

"La vision du passé: ce qu'elle apporte a la science et ce qu'elle lui ôte," *Études,* 263 (1949), 308–15; *Colloques des sciences de la terre* (ed. by J. Privetau), Paris: Hermann, 1950, pp. 71–74; *La vision du passé,* pp. 333–43.

1950. "Les australopithèques et le chainon manquant (ou missing link) de l'évolution," *Études,* 265 (1950), 340–45; *L'apparition de l'homme,* pp. 175–83.

"Le phénomène Chrétien."

"Réflexions sur l'ultra-humain — ou les phase d'une planète vivante."

"Le cœur de la matière."

"Évolution et l'idée d'évolution," *Bulletin de l'Union Catholique des Scientifiques Français* (June–July, 1950); *La vision du passé,* pp. 345–50.

"Sur un cas remarquable d'orthogénèse de groupe: l'évolution des Siphneides de Chine," *Paléontologie et Transformisme,* Paris, 1950. Pp. 169–73.

1951. "Notes de préhistoire Sud-Africaine"; *L'apparition de l'homme,* 235–42.

"La convergence de l'univers."

"Du cosmos à la cosmogénèse" (March 15).

"Le paléolithique du Siam," *L'anthropologie,* 54 (1951), 547–49.

"Note sur le réalité actuelle et la signification évolutive d'une orthogénèse humain" (Paris, May 5); *La vision du passé,* pp. 351–62.

"La structure phylétique du groupe humain," *Annales de paléontologie,* 37 (1951); *L'apparition de l'homme,* pp. 185–234.

1952. "On the Zoological Position and the Evolutionary Significance of Australopithecines," *Transactions of the New York Academy of Sciences,* ser. 2, vol. 14, no. 5, pp. 208–10; *Yearbook of Physical Anthropology,* 8 (1952), 37–39; "Observations sur les Australopithécinés," *L'apparition de l'homme,* pp. 249–55.

"On the Biological Meaning of Human Socialization."

"Hominisation et spéciation," *Revue scientifique,* 90 (1952), 434–38; *La vision du passé,* pp. 363–79.

"La place de l'homme dans l'univers," (Peking, November 15); *La vision du passé,* pp. 303–26.

"La réflexion de l'énergie," *Revue des questions scientifiques,* 13 (1952), 481–97.

1953. "Sur la probabilité d'une bifurcation précoce du phylum humain au voisinage immédiat de ses origines," *Compte rendu des séances, Académie des Sciences,* 237 (1953), 1293–94; *L'apparition de l'homme,* pp. 257–61.

"Australopithèques pithécanthropes et structure phylétiques des hominiens," *Compte rendu séances, Académie des Sciences,* 237 (1953), 377–79; *L'apparition de l'homme,* pp. 243–48.

"Contingence de l'univers et goût humain de survivre."

"Réflexions sur la compression humaine" (November).

"En regard un cyclotron: réflexion sur le reploiement sur soi de l'énergie humain," *Recherches et Débats, pensée scientifiques et foi chrétienne,* 1953.

"La fin d'espèce," *Psyché* (February, 1953), 81–7.

"The Idea of Fossil Man," *Anthropology Today: An Encyclopedic Inventory.* By A. L. KROEBER et al. Chicago: University of Chicago, 1953. Pp. 93–100.

1954. "Les singularités de l'espèce humain" (March 24), *Annales de paléontologie,* 41 (1955), 3–52; *L'apparition de l'homme,* pp. 293–374 (with an appendix, "Remarques sur la nature du Point Oméga ou De la singularité du phénomène chrétien," hitherto unpublished).

"Les recherches pour la découverte des origines humaines en Afrique au sud du Sahara," *L'anthropologie,* 58 (1954), 74–78; *L'apparition de l'homme,* pp. 263–73.

"Un sommaire de ma perspective 'phénoménologique' du monde."

"Un sommaire de ma Weltanschauung."

"L'Afrique et les origines humaines" (September), *Revue des questions scientifiques,* 16 (1955), 5–17; *L'apparition de l'homme,* 275–91.

1955. "Le Christique" (March).

Review of *Problématique de l'évolution* in *Études,* 285 (1955), 279.

"Une défense de l'orthogénèse à propos des figures de spéciation" (January); *La vision du passé,* pp. 381–91.

1956. *L'apparition de l'homme.* Paris: Seuil, 1956.

1957. *La vision du passé.* Paris: Seuil, 1957.

1958. *Construire la terre,* / *Building the Earth,* / *Die Erde Aufbauen* / etc. Paris: Seuil, 1958.

Undated. "Un front humain spirituel"; *La table ronde,* 90 (1955), 55–59.

"Note sur le Christ universel."

"Christologie et évolution."

"Monogénisme et monophylétisme."

2. About Teilhard de Chardin

Anonymous. "La carrière scientifique du P. Teilhard de Chardin," *Études,* 226 (1950), 126–28.

————. "P. Teilhard de Chardin," *Tablet,* 205 (1955), 394.

ARAGONNES, C. (M. TEILHARD DE CHAMBON). "Le voyageur et l'explorateur," *La table ronde,* 90 (1955), 25–28.

ARMAGNAC, C. D'. "Philosophie de la nature et méthode chez la P. Teilhard de Chardin," *Archives de philosophie,* 20 (1957), 5–41.

BEGOUEN, M.-H. "1915, au front avec Teilhard de Chardin," *La table ronde,* 90 (1955), 60–63.

BERNOVILLE, G. "Contemporary Trends in Catholic Thought in France," *Dublin Review,* 224 (1950), 20–22.

BONE, E. "Pierre Teilhard de Chardin, S.J.," *Revue des questions scientifiques,* 17 (5th ser.) (1956), 90–104.

————. Review of *L'apparition de l'homme* and *La vision du passé* in *Nouvelle revue théologique,* 79 (1957), 984–85.

BOROS, L. "Evolutionismus und Anthropologie," *Wort und Wahrheit,* 13 (1958), 15–24.

BOSCIO, G. "Il fenomeno umano nell' ipotesi dell' evoluzione integrale," *Civiltà cattolica,* 106, IV (Dec. 17, 1955), 622 ff.; *L'Osservatore Romano,* Dec. 23, 1955; "Le phénomène humain dans l'hypothèse de l'évolution intégrale," *Documentation Catholique,* Jan. 22, 1956.

BREUIL, H. "Les enquêtes du géologue et du préhistorien," *La table ronde,* 90 (1955), 19–24.

COGNET, L. *Le Père Teilhard de Chardin et la pensée contemporaine.* Paris: Flammarion, 1952.

CORTE, N. *La vie et l'âme de Teilhard de Chardin.* Paris: Fayard, 1957.

CUENOT, C. *Pierre Teilhard de Chardin: Les grandes étapes de son évolution.* Paris: Plon, 1958.

————. "Teilhard de Chardin et les philosophies," *La table ronde,* 90 (1955), 36–40.

D'ARCY, M. C. "The Varieties of Human Love," *Saturday Evening Post,* 231 (1959), 38 ff.

DELCOURT, A. "À propos de Teilhard: la vision scientifique du monde," *Revue nouvelle,* 27 (1958), 591–610.

DEVINE, W. "Scientist Missionaries in China," *Irish Ecclesiastical Record,* 36 (1930), 136–43.

DORGET, L. "1941, à Pékin," *La table ronde,* 90 (1955), 76.

DUBARLE, D. "Église et chrétienté: à propos du *Phénomène humain* du P. Teilhard de Chardin," *La vie intellectuelle,* 27 (1956), 6–25.

GALOT, J., *"Le phénomène humain*: à propos d'un livre recent," *Nouvelle revue théologique,* 78 (1956), 177–82.

GARROD, D. A. E. "Pierre Teilhard de Chardin, 1881–1955," *Man,* 55 (1955), 70.

GEORGE, A. "Pour le Père Teilhard de Chardin," *La table ronde,* 90 (1955), 77–80.

GEX, M. "Vers un humanisme cosmologique. La synthèse de Teilhard de Chardin," *Revue de théologie et philosophie,* 7 (N.S.) (1957), 187–206.

GIBLET, J. "La vision chrétienne de l'univers," *Revue nouvelle,* 27 (1958), 611–22.

HOLSTEIN, H. Review of *Nouvelles lettres de voyage (1939–1955)* in *Études,* 297 (1958), 274.

IRIARTE, J. "Al dimidiar este gran siglo nuestro: Lombardi, Przywara, Teilhard de Chardin," *Razón y Fe,* 154 (1956), 77 ff.

JACOB, A. "Ein neuer Fall Galilei?," *Frankreich Geistiges,* 7 (1953), 1–4.

JACOB, C. "Notice sur la vie et l'œuvre scientifique du P. Teilhard de Chardin," *La table ronde,* 90 (1955), 15–18.

JOURNET, C. Review of *Le milieu divin* in *Nova et vetera,* July–September, 1958.

KNODEL, A. "An Introduction to the Integral Evolutionism of Teilhard de Chardin," *Personalist,* 38 (1957), 347–55.

LAWLER, J. G. "Chardin and Human Knowledge," *Commonweal,* 68 (1958), 40–49.

LE BLOND, J.-M. "Consacrer l'effort humain," *Études*, 296 (1958), 58–68.

LEROY, P. *Pierre Teilhard de Chardin tel que je l'ai connu*. Paris: Plon, 1958.

MCNASPY, C. "A Theology of History?", *Worship*, 32 (1958), 464–9.

MALEVEZ, L. "La méthode du P. Teilhard de Chardin et la phénoménologie," *Nouvelle revue théologique*, 79 (1957), 579–99.

MARTINDALE, C. C. Letter to *Tablet*, 205 (1955), 460.

MOLITOR, A. "Bibliographie sommaire," *Revue nouvelle*, 27 (1958), 623–24.

MONFRIED, H. DE. "1922, en mer Rouge," *La table ronde*, 90, (1955), 68–71.

MOVIUS, H. L. Jr. "Pierre Teilhard de Chardin, Paleoanthropologist," *Science*, 123 (1956), 92.

————. "Pierre Teilhard de Chardin, S.J., 1881–1955," *American Anthropologist*, 58 (1956), 147–50.

OUY, A. "Sint ut sunt" (review of *Le Père Teilhard de Chardin et la pensée contemporaine* by L. COGNET), *Mercure de France*, 316 (1952), 366 ff.

PIVETEAU, J. "L'histoire de la vie et l'origine des espèces," *La table ronde*, 90 (1955), 31–35.

POULAIN, D. "Christ and the Universe," *Commonweal*, 69 (1959), 460–64.

RABUT, O. A. *Dialogue avec Teilhard de Chardin*. Paris: Cerf, 1958.

ROCHEFOUCAULD, E. DE LA. "1928, à Paris, réncontre avec le Pierre Teilhard de Chardin," *La table ronde*, 90 (1955), 72–75.

RUSSO, F. "Actualités, Le Père Pierre Teilhard de Chardin," *Études*, 285 (1955), 254–59.

————. "Autour d'une pensée contestée," *Études*, 300 (1959), 118–20.

————. Review of *Lettres de voyage (1923–1939)* in *Études*, 290 (1956), 305.

SCHLUETES-HERMKES, M. "Der Mensch: Sinn der Evolution," *Hochland*, 51 (1958), 115 ff.

SEGAAR, E. and CHARBONEAU, B. "À propos du P. Teilhard de Chardin," *Foe et vie*, November-December, 1957.

SOLAGES, B. DE. "La pensée chrétienne face a l'évolution," *Bulletin de litterature ecclesiastique*, 48 (1947), 103–116; "Christianity and Evolution," *Cross Currents*, 4 (1951), 26–37.

TANNEGUY DE QUENETAIN, M. "Un livre qui bouleverse notre vision du monde," *Réalites,* September, 1956.

TOWERS, B. "Significance of Teilhard de Chardin," *Blackfriars,* 40 (1959), 126–29.

TRESMONTANT, C. "Note sur l'œuvre de Teilhard de Chardin," *Études philosophique,* 10 (1955), 602, 604.

_____. "Pierre Teilhard de Chardin," *Revue nouvelle,* 21 (1955), 614–27.

VIALLET, F. A. " 'Amor terrae' Pierre Teilhard de Chardin, ein Kunder neuen Weltgefuhls," *Antares,* 4 (1956), 14–18.

_____. *L'univers personnel de Teilhard de Chardin.* Paris: Amicot-Dumont, 1955.

_____. "Versuch eines personlichen Universums," *Abendland,* 10 (1955), 565–67.

VILLAIN, J. "*Le phénomène humain* de Père de Chardin," *Études,* 287 (1955), 401–03.

WEINER, J. S. *The Piltdown Forgery.* New York: Oxford, 1955.

WILDIERS, N. M. "L'experience fondamentale du Pierre Teilhard de Chardin," *La table ronde,* 90 (1955), 41–54.

Indíces

1. Index of Teilhardian Texts Cited

"Âme du monde, L'," 98
"Centrologie," 14, 45, 58
"Christique, Le," 76
"Cœur de la matière, Le," 7, 18, 31, 38, 55, 57, 58, 76, 80, 86, 88, 93
"Cœur du problème, Le," 36, 39, 72, 82, 83
"Comment je crois," 48, 71, 81, 89, 90
"Comment je vois," 52, 73, 77, 91, 93, 95, 98
"Contingence de l'univers et goût humain de survivre," 93
"Du cosmos a la cosmogénèse," 31
"Énergie humain, L'," 45, 46, 55, 56, 61, 62, 85
"Esprit de la terre, L'," 46, 48, 61, 62
"Esquisse d'un univers personnel," 13, 21, 22, 30, 60
"Groupe zoologique humain, Le," 19, 24, 26, 29, 32, 33, 34
"Hominisation, L'," 9, 13
"Interprétation plausible de l'histoire humaine: la formation de la Noosphère," 60
"Lutte contre la multitude, La," 90, 91
"Maîtrise du monde, La," 45, 80
Milieu divin, Le, 5, 76, 80, 85, 86
"Mon univers," 7
"Noms de la matière, Les," 91
"Note sur la notion de perfection chrétienne," 83, 84

"Note sur les modes de l'action divine dans l'univers," 96
"Paléontologie et l'apparition de l'homme, La," 2
Phénomène humain, Le, 5, 6, 14, 20, 21, 22, 23, 24, 33, 34, 40, 42, 52, 56, 57, 59, 77, 87
"Place de l'homme dans l'univers, réflexions sur la complexité, La," 14, 20, 24, 25, 26, 54
"Rebondissement humain de l'évolution et ses conséquences, Le," 38, 43, 45, 47
"Réflexion de l'énergie, La," 16, 40, 41, 42, 43, 46, 52, 53
"Réflexions sur l'ultra-humain," 20, 21, 41
"Résumé de la pensée du Père," 15
Review of *Problématique de l'évolution*, 17
"Sommaire de ma Weltanschauung, Un," 23
"Structure phylétique du groupe humain, La," 35, 37, 41, 43, 44, 53
"Super-humanité," 29, 33, 71, 75
"Union créatrice, L'," 51, 74, 90, 92
"Vie cosmique, La," 13, 36, 54, 73, 74, 79, 80, 97
"Vie et planètes," 14, 25, 26, 27, 28, 32

2. Index of Persons

Abraham the Patriarch, 88
Anaxagoras, 91
Aristotle, 17, 50, 69, 91
Augustine of Hippo, St., 38, 80, 106
Bergson, Henri, 6, 40, 50–51, 60

Blondel, Maurice, 42
Boehme, Jacob, 94
Calvin, John, 77
Chrysippus, 69
Des Bosses, Bartholomew, 8

Descartes, René, 96, 104
Einstein, Albert, 100
Freud, Sigmund, 78, 82
Galileo Galilei, 18, 100
Gregory of Nyssa, St., 106
Hegel, Georg Wilhelm Friedrich, 94
Heidegger, Martin, 44
Huxley, Julian, 38, 40
Irenaeus of Lyons, St., 38, 84, 95, 106
John Duns Scotus, 97
John of the Cross, St., 88
John the Evangelist, St., 36, 73, 75
Kant, Immanuel, 91
Laberthonnière, L., 50
Leibniz, Gottfried Wilhelm, 5, 6, 8, 96, 97
Le Roy, Édouard, 9, 13, 40
Marx, Karl, 44, 78, 82, 95
Meyer, François, 17, 21, 99

Mounier, Emmanuel, 49
Nietzsche, Friedrich Wilhelm, 78, 82
Pascal, Blaise, 29, 38, 95
Paul the Apostle, St., 36, 70, 73–74, 85, 86, 93, 97, 106
Pelagius, 84
Piveteau, Jean, 3
Plato, 69, 92
Plotinus, 50–51
Pontius Pilate, 76
"P.T.," 79
Schelling, Friedrich Wilhelm Joseph von, 5, 94
Solages, Bruno de, 16–17, 62, 99
Spinoza, Baruch, 50
Teilhard de Chardin, Pierre, *passim*
Teresa of Ávila, St., 88
Thomas Aquinas, St., 19
Tresmontant, Claude, 20